ALEXANDRA YORK

FROM THE FOUNTAINHEAD
TO THE FUTURE

and Other Essays on Art and Excellence

SILVER ROSE PRESS
an imprint of
ART

AMERICAN RENAISSANCE FOR THE
TWENTY-FIRST CENTURY, INC.
NEW YORK, NY

an imprint of
ART

AMERICAN RENAISSANCE
FOR THE TWENTY-FIRST CENTURY, INC.
F.D.R. STATION, P.O. BOX 8379, NEW YORK, NY 10150-1919

ART is a 501(c)(3) nonprofit educational foundation dedicated to a
rebirth of beauty and
life-affirming values in all of the fine arts.

Web site: www. art-21.org
E-mail: ARTinfo@art-21.org

ISBN 0-9676444-0-2

Book cover design by Kenneth J. Smith, Smith Communications
Artworks reproduced with permission of the following artists:
Reaching, by EvAngelos Frudakis; *Spring at Crescent Pond,* by Richard
Whitney; *Sea of Dreams,* by Samuel Knecht; *Four Horses,* by Elisabeth
Gordon Chandler; *Nearing the Bend,* by Peter Adams; *Dance!,* by Marc
Mellon, *Awakening of Eve,* by Frederick E. Hart(© 1994 F. Hart).

*This book is dedicated to those
like-minded souls who, in Victor Hugo's words, "...dream
to create the future."*

June 10, 2004

To Aldon James,

Thank you for your
support of our deeply
shared values.

Alexandra York

Acknowledgements

I wish to thank those whose time and good efforts helped put this volume together: Barrett Randell, Irene Pierpont, Matt Fontana, Pierre Rioux, Jeff Britting, Del Marbrook, Marilyn Marbrook and Ken Smith. I also thank Joseph Veach Noble for writing the Foreword to the book, thereby adding his own fine sense of truth and beauty to the endeavor.

In addition, I would like to thank every member of the American Renaissance for the Twenty-first Century, Inc. foundation from its inception to tomorrow, for our members are the strength of our achievements.

ART's Board of Advisors, who are crucial to the leadership of the foundation, are listed here with my gratitude and ever abiding admiration: EvAngelous Frudakis, Elisabeth Gordon Chandler, Richard Whitney, Samuel Knecht, John Massaro, Rudolph Schirmer, Frederick Clifford Gibson, Roslyn Targ, William Edward Baer, Jeff Britting, Gail Dubinbaum, William Greene, Diana Brill, Donald Martin Reynolds, Marc Mellon, Peter Adams, and in memoriam, Fredrick E. Hart and Elizabeth de C. Wilson.

Foreword

Many people think that art is an elusive subject, fluttering about like a butterfly; therefore, anyone who tries to pin it down by writing about it faces a daunting challenge. Alexandra York has seized this opportunity of expressing her analyses, judgments and hopes for the art of today. She has done this through her essays, which are insightful and thought-provoking.

The author has bravely faced many controversial issues and expressed her ideas clearly. At a period in history when nonsense art pollutes the world, it is helpful that Alexandra York calls junk just that and urges everyone of higher aspirations to enjoy, admire and collect real art of beauty and meaning. For this we are indebted to her.

Now, it is up to the reader to respond to the values that permeate this lively volume of work. Many of us will applaud the art and ideas she supports, but even if one disagrees, her words are both timely and timeless—well worth consideration. Whatever one's persuasion, we all can be thankful that she has pinned down the butterfly of art for each of us to examine.

Joseph Veach Noble
Director Emeritus, Museum of the City of New York;
former Vice Director, the Metropolitan Museum of Art;
past President, American Association of Museums

Preface

This small volume is in response to a large and growing number of people who have requested that certain of my work be collected into one publication. The essays and speeches included herein were written between the years 1992 and 1999. The "American Renaissance for the Twenty-first Century" (ART) foundation was founded in 1992, obtained its 501(c)(3) IRS status as a nonprofit educational foundation in 1993, and began publishing its quarterly magazine *ART Ideas* in 1994. Some of the work included appeared in "My Word" editorials for that publication, some were given as speeches in one venue or another, while still others were essays that appeared in various publications or in the catalogues of art exhibits produced by the ART foundation.

As with any compilation, the reader will find numerous cases of repetition both in quotations cited and ideas explored. When this occurs it is because the audience for any given piece was different, providing a new opportunity to offer certain quotes and observations which I feel are so pertinent, succinct and empowering that, anew or repeated, they cannot be heard often enough. Too, I consider certain *ideas* to be so worthy for contemplation that I chose to come at them several times over but from a variety of angles in order to limn their significance. For these reasons—even though each was written as a one-time-only effort—these works are presented unedited, except for some errant typos and a few passages that I felt were unclear or could be misconstrued.

The essays can be read in the order presented (which is not always the order in which they were written, for reasons of subject or venue continuity) or—in my mind a better program—the reader may pick and choose at will. Please note, however, that all works are dated and the form of their original delivery noted to provide chronology and context should the reader desire it.

Although each piece was written for a general audience, I had two segments of the population that I especially wanted to reach because of the unnatural chasm dividing them: individuals who are extraordinarily facile with ideas but not with the art that expresses them—this sadly includes philosophers—and individuals who are extraordinarily facile with art and aesthetics but who do not understand the values that inspire them—this sadly includes artists.

The underlying theme of my writing during this *fin de siècle* decade rests on my certainty that although we live in a morally and spiritually turbulent culture—where nihilism and political correctness have become mainstream—the time is ripe for philosophically inspired art to emerge from our midst like "homing" search lights beamed onto viable paths that might lead us out of our present morass into the natural sunlight of a tomorrow where people will have learned again to cherish beauty and rational values.

The stated mission of the American Renaissance for the Twenty-first Century (ART) foundation is to promote a rebirth of beauty and life-affirming values in all of the fine arts. It is to this end that all of my efforts over the past many years have been specifically dedicated—championing the artists who create beautiful, uplifting art and offering not only their artistic visions but also the ideas that inform their work to every individual who finds enjoyment in art and embarks on the blissful task of contemplating it for the purpose of enriching his or her own daily life via the joy and hope that such art embodies.

It is my fervent hope and my well-studied belief that every crisis is not necessarily a catastrophe and that, in fact, most crises (cultural or personal) actually afford grand opportunities to look freshly at problems and devise enlightened methods to solve them. If only one of my works were to be read, I should choose "*The Legacy Lives: Embracing the Year Three Thousand*," for it provides a wide lens through which one may view our current cultural maladies as well as an exploration into at least some of the various possibilities available to us to create solutions redressing them. "The Fountainhead," of course, is philosophy as first identified in ancient Greece and "The Future" will be charted by (to quote that essay) "those of us who will gather together the vision, the courage, the energy and the talent so abundant among us to open a new, clear channel through which our reborn values can flow from the fountainhead to the future and, in its wake, create the surging, shining wave of a genuine, lasting American Renaissance in art and ideas that will rise to take its place among the high watermarks of human history."

Alexandra York
New York City
January 2000

Contents

If of thy mortal goods thou art bereft
And from thy slender store
Two loaves alone to thee are left
Sell one, and with the dole
Buy hyacinths to feed thy soul

Muslih-uddin Sadi
Thirteenth-Century Persian poet

From the Fountainhead to the Future: Charting the course to an American Renaissance in Art and Ideas

First published in the Premiere issue of ART Ideas, *Spring 1994.*

**"He who has access to the fountain
does not go to the waterpot."**

The above quote from Leonardo da Vinci sums up not only what the first Renaissance leaders did but also what we in America must do. The fountain? Now, as in Leonardo's time: Ancient Greece and the prototype of the human ideal.

It is my conviction that in order to engender an all encompassing American Renaissance, we, too, must begin, as did the ancient Greeks, with the moral and spiritual nourishment of the individual, the "undivided" self. Individual excellence of personal character, of physical fitness and of spiritual wholeness *was* the Greek ideal. Further, it was the Greek thesis that individuals striving toward this ideal would, by virtue of the striving alone, create a diverse yet mutually beneficial society. And further, it was their novel idea that art could be wrested from its primitive origins and usages to become a universal language with the power to communicate abstract, philosophical ideas via concrete forms that speak directly to all individuals *as* individuals. How right they were! Still today, in a vastly altered world, their great art uplifts the spirits of people all over the globe, reminding us each of the beauty, the possibilities and the glories of human potential.

For most of America's short history, we held ideals of individual excellence similar to those of our philosophical ancestors. But by the early mid-twentieth century, individualism—following the European paradigm of angst—began to turn into rampant subjectivity; individual liberty (bereft of responsibility) turned into license; moral principles turned into pragmatism; tolerance turned into permissiveness; and (most) art turned into an excuse for emotional purging, political activism and the enshrinement of wanton violence and human degradation. In art, Duchamp became the lingering muse: objective standards of judgment were ridiculed; anything and everything was called art if an "artist" said it was and got one critic to agree. Predictably, self-proclaimed twentieth century American iconoclasts (again following their European models) became nihilists, as all must do when promulgating the annihilation of cherished values and ideals without offering better ones to replace them.

Today, as we approach the end of this century, we who would set our feet upon a path to a renaissance of high culture face strong opposing forces already well entrenched and hard at work to further debase our culture. There are many in the country who would return us to a period of "Bread and Circuses" at best or an era of primitivism, tribalism, collectivism, occultism and all manner of escape from reality (and responsibility) at worst. There are many also bent on creating divisions where none need exist: between black and white, between men and women, between mind and body, reason and emotion, art and meaning. Raw sensationalism pervades TV, movies, the visual arts, popular fiction, music and sex, as it must in the absence of values. The media mongers trip over each other in their rush to explore the souls of serial killers, rapists and child molesters, but few even think to explore the souls of heros, creators and achievers. We live in an age that is emotionally conflicted, and much of our art and most of our institutions reflect this conflict. Without valid values as guides, we are offered the false alternatives of emotional indulgence or emotional denial, encouraged either to let our feelings run hot and wild without the restraint of reason or else accept reason sterilized into a cold rigid formalism that anesthetizes feelings; look to contemporary music for especially salient examples.

But let us not despair! If nothing else, the destruction has been so devastating that a new path may now be cleared to redirect our culture toward re-examined and redefined values. In order to gain energy for the charting of a new map from the ideological starting point, however, we need fuel—emotional fuel. This means nurturing not only the mind, but the heart and the soul as well. This means championing beautiful and life-affirming art and the ideas that inspire it. Or to put it in reverse, we must champion rational, life-affirming values and the art that expresses them, for fine art *is* values made physically manifest. In a society where increasingly militant group identity causes polarity, we must seek commonality among individuals who share universal values and eternal truths that hold for all humankind. In a time when "decaditis" is fracturing contemporary history literally into ten-year bits, we must honor timeless verities. In an artistic climate that glorifies ugliness, we must revere beauty.

Beauty: Order. Proportion. Balance. Harmony. Grace. Beauty possesses redemptive powers all of its own, as in nature. But when beauty is created by human hand, it can be even more redemptive, more powerful, because it is created with intent. In their elevated art forms (beyond utilitarian function and decor), some expressions of beauty are also permeated with the highest of human values, letting each of us, individually, experience our own best self as surely as if our own soul were turned inside out and visible to us reflected clearly and sharply from a mirror. Mathematical beauty can become an end in itself in art as exemplified by the best abstract sculpture and painting; but this is not the highest purpose of art because it lacks human content. Nor is beauty, per se, the *raison d'etre* of high art—"high art" is here defined as art expressing such a depth and universality of humanistic meaning that it transcends not only its local subject matter but also its own time and place and becomes a projection of a heightened reality; thus, it acquires metaphysical relevance and the power to strike a spiritually sympathetic chord in the very center of our beings *qua* human beings. In short, high art, in addition to an expression of aesthetic values, communicates timeless and universal human values.

Beauty can be, however, the "charm," the form, the vehicle that incites the "aesthetic arrest" in us, immediately capturing our rapt attention while delivering deeper messages in slower tempo for our inner contemplation. Beauty, then, can exist in many forms both natural and man-made without being high art, but high art cannot exist without beauty of form. Beauty can be both physical and mental; it can be both an identification and an evaluation; this is why beauty and truth dovetail so perfectly, why the greatest art is both beautiful and true: art and ideas. In Western heritage art forms, this means representationalism in the visual arts, tonality and melody in music, grace and intelligible expressiveness of movement in dance, and the reverberating interaction of structure, rhythm and meaning in written works, all of which afford artists an immensely rich vocabulary for unlimited communication through the combined power—via a supremely thoughtful integrative process—of both aesthetic and metaphorical means.

Sight, touch, sound and intellection—not to mention the mysterious and wondrous realm of the imagination—can all be stimulated and satisfied through these art forms because the forms themselves are malleable and limitless; they can stretch, bend, twist, turn, expand and reduce to accommodate endless meanings. In humanistic art, form (physical presentation) always serves content (ideas and values). The attributes of beauty reside inherently in the human form and in the forms of the natural world. Beauty can be found also in the integration of harmonies and the variations in melodies, in the order and complexities of rhythms, in textures and colors—all variously shaped by human intention into images and sounds that stir recognition, aesthetic pleasure and emotional-intellectual connection. These same art forms, of course, can be distorted and made dissonant to serve perfectly proper artistic purposes, but to turn beauty against itself for the conscious purpose of deliberately offending human sensibilities and to defile the human figure, as is being done in too much art today, is to display a hatred not only for art but for life itself.

Those of us who love life and the art that enhances living must seek out other like-minded individuals and join together in camaraderie and good will to enjoy and enrich our moments on this earth through art experiences that lift up our spirits, move us to contemplative thought and remind us why life is worth living. Painters, sculptors, writers, composers, dancers, musicians, actors, poets, audiences, patrons. All! We not only need to write about ideas but also to promote the showing of ideas in all their various and captivating forms through the only tangible means possible other than science: *art*. Indeed, in a society becoming more illiterate by the minute, art may be the one dynamic powerful enough to envision for us a way to a better future.

The success of the Renaissance Europeans lay in the fact that they did not attempt to repeat the Greek ideal. They reached back to Greece, as we must now do, only to create a true rebirth of ideas that they then made manifest, as did the Greeks themselves, through their own great art. They redefined the Greek ideal to suit their own needs, to express their own context—David, not Apollo. Now, it is our turn. What will the next millennium heroes and heroines look like? As we approach the beginning of this momentous turn of a century, we who seek the way to a better tomorrow must dedicate ourselves today to those human values that express the best within us in order to usher in a future culture that can outshine even the Golden Ages of the past. And how better to express "the best within us" than through works of art that project the world at its most beautiful and man and woman in their most noble state?

The following quote (from an unknown source) seems pertinent here:

> Pre-renaissance nostalgia was not self indulgent
> and debilitating, but turned into a vigorous and

> revitalizing current which inspired writers, artists and craftsmen to give expression to the new mood...

Obviously written in reference to the Italian phenomenon, the notion of a "new mood" resonates particularly well today. If we look carefully, we can glimpse, as if wafting up like a fine mist from the troubled waters of our age, a rising concern for individual liberty in certain political sectors and a resurgence of a romantic spirit in certain of the arts. It may just be that a faint scent of the perfume of hope is in the air. Most definitely, our own desires to renew the values of beauty, humanism and the moral ideal should not be mere "nostalgia" for the past but a "vigorous" commitment to the future. We should desire to create a rallying point of view that includes all of the fine arts. We should desire to establish and support places and organizations where kindred spirits may learn about each other and combine efforts toward a common vision of fresh expressions of individualism and the beauties of the world in which we live. We should support venues where the art of contemporary artists who express these life-serving values in their work may be promoted and brought to national awareness—"contemporary" meaning living artists, not a particular art persuasion (!). Our attitude of devotion to ethos should not deny pathos, but it must emphasize the tenet that human struggle and suffering can become acts of affirmation by projecting visions of why the struggle is worthwhile. We cannot salve (nor solve) the sorrows of humankind by continually lamenting over what is wrong; we must hold up what is right. It is wasteful to fight against; it is productive to fight for. Ours should be a declarative step toward establishing a nationwide, cooperative endeavor to create a rebirth (not a revival) of positive art and ideas that will give "expression to the new mood...vigorous and revitalizing."

There is no doubt that we live in a dangerous but exhilarating time. The prize is great but the stakes are high, for if we do not generate another Renaissance, then surely we shall suffer the default position of another Dark Age. The art and ideas that we of a positive and humanistic persuasion choose to champion must be expressions not of division but of integration: mind, body and soul in harmony, passions elicited from value stimulation rather than sensory titillation, and brotherhood born from shared values rather than color, creed, gender or bloodline. Those of us who understand the philosophical premises expressed through art are charged with far more than a simplistic call for a return to beauty or a poignant cry for a lost innocence that never existed. We are charged with the more profound responsibility of giving expression to a deeper mood...one of renewed celebration— a mood that seeks not to escape reality but to embrace it, celebrating the joys, the hopes and the possibilities of life. Human life. We can curse the darkness as we should and do, but that will not be constructive unless we also draw back the curtain and let in the light.

Art imbued with beauty that expresses life-serving values and humanistic ideas (and ideals) is a potent manifestation of that light, the same philosophical flame ignited in ancient Greece, rekindled during the European Renaissance and the Enlightenment and reflected across all civilizations ever since in a myriad of forms that celebrate individual achievement and excellence. America was founded as the political incarnation of that light. Let us now, like Olympians who celebrate the wonders of physical excellence through sport, lift the torch high and illuminate the way to celebrate the wonders of a spiritual renewal through art. As we approach the coming millennium, let us join together and gather the vision, the courage, the energy and the talent so abundant among us to open a new, clear channel through which our reborn values can flow from the fountainhead to the future, and in its wake, create the surging, shining wave of a genuine, lasting American Renaissance in art and ideas that will rise to take its place among the high watermarks of human history.

There are moments in our lives, there are moments in a day, when we seem to see beyond the usual. Such are the moments of our greatest happiness. Such are the moments of our greatest wisdom. If one could but recall his vision by some sort of sign. It was in this hope that the arts were invented. Sign-posts on the way to what may be. Sign-posts toward greater knowledge.

Robert Henri

In Search of the Ideal

First published in ART Ideas, *Autumn 1994*
and *Winter 1995, in two parts.*

B efore any one of us sets out on a journey, we must have
at least some mind's eye vision of our destination,
whether it's the corner grocery store or the North Pole. Life,
for each of us, is made up of a series of journeys to a variety
of destinations, some physical places or professional plateaus
to be reached, others intellectual or personal goals to be
achieved. If an *ideal* can be said to be a "destination" of sorts
toward which one individual or a whole country can journey,
then surely, over the last half of the twentieth century, we
have lost our way as a nation for lack of the "mind's eye
vision" that would keep us headed in the right direction.
Without some sort of mental "picture" of contemporary
human excellence toward which we can strive, we are left
wandering and wondering why. We are also left at the mercy
of every passerby who, claiming to know "the Way," wishes
to lead us unawares down obscure alleys toward destinations
we might rather not reach. Therefore it is crucial to define
for ourselves, in the form of ideals projected in our mind's
eye, visions of men and women fit to survive the reality of a
twenty-first-century world. Since an ideal is a supreme
summation of mental value judgments, the most immediately
apprehensible physical form through which to communicate
or confirm our evaluated abstract ideas are works of art in
all their various and metaphorical guises.

Ideas are what brought ancient Greece—and the resulting
idealized art—to greatness. The same holds true for the
European Renaissance. The opportunity for advancement
in the humanities repeats itself today. In a culture where so
many are focused on the "dark side" of life, those of us
concerned with positive, life-affirming values may offer fresh
ideas projecting redefined, contemporary images of human
excellence that might assist in the journey out from our

present "black hole" of a culture into the sunlit, wide-open spaces of tomorrow. Victor Hugo said, "There is nothing like dream to create the future." So let us dream together and seek visions of the future human ideal.

We can define the ideal broadly as a purposefully formulated mental construct, meaning a consciously selected and particularly arranged combination of concepts—an awake "dream"—that projects excellence in the sense of a perfectly realized potential which is, in principle, possible to achieve. We must reject at the outset the notion of "the impossible dream" but accept the requisite of a rational dream. It is only when the ideal is "idealized" to the point of becoming a utopian fantasy of the *idyll* (a poetically appealing but Arcadian image of reality) or the *idol* (an image without substance to be worshiped blindly) that the dream becomes impossible. Fulfillment of such irrational dreams *is* impossible, not because dreams *per se* are unattainable but because dreams such as these are false. Conversely, rational ideals composed of values selected under the guidance of reason that are in harmony with the real world and with the nature of real human beings are not only achievable but necessary. * Rational ideals, in fact, serve highly practical purposes: visions of reality-oriented yet inspirational ideals may serve both as distant suns to be sought or as beacons to illuminate the way to those suns on our inner, spiritual paths in the same way that towns and mountains, as landmarks or end destinations, determine the roads we will follow on our physical journeys. Whether mileposts to be passed or ultimate goals, *ideals are destinations of the soul*.

Art is the unique medium through which we may experience our mental ideals by establishing images in our minds eye—like a town or a mountain—of where we are going on the journey to our own best selves. Ideals expressed through art are not projections of the superhuman but of the significant. They appear larger than life in art only because existential details must be eliminated in order to present abstract values in a pure, unencumbered yet readily accessible form. The ideal as projected in art is neither the everyday nor the episodic; it is stripped of journalistic and naturalistic attributes down to its bare essentials for the purpose of concretizing the abstract ideas that inspire its creation in concentrated form. It is in a very real sense a frozen form of ideas.

But towns and mountains, one might observe, exist "out there" in reality. These are directly perceivable destinations, physical entities that can be viewed, described and visited— an accurate observation and one which aptly illustrates the crucial function of art to translate our "in here" spiritual "destinations" into concrete forms. Since we cannot perceive abstract ideas and values directly through the evidence of our senses, art can provide us with the physical, sensorily accessible manifestations of our mental concepts; art *can* be viewed, described and visited. Art lets us "be there" in person, *experiencing* our values. By speaking of ideals as destinations we mean, of course, not only destinations to be approached—"distant suns to be sought" or "beacons to illuminate the way"—but also destinations to be confirmed, spotlights on goals reached.

If our value system is rational, consistent and integrated (the result of arduous intellectual effort) and we are living out our values to the fullest capacity through our actions, *then* when presented with our ideals in directly perceivable form (as through art), we are rewarded by the ultimate emotional experience of *self-celebration*. The exquisite joy of moments such as these is an end in itself, reflecting the pure exultation of individual accomplishment as if from the intense beam of an inner light shining on an earned self-fulfillment that becomes a salute. If we are still "on our way" to our best self not yet realized in existential life, then an inspiring value experience through art that "shows" us our desired ideals can act to spur us on with renewed energy, which encourages us to stretch ourselves even further in our intellectual and personal development. In either case, whether a moment of inspiration or one of celebration, the ideal in art is always experienced in the immediate "now." Even though there may be self realization of the ideal yet to be achieved in our actual lives, there is no feeling of unfinished business or yearning at that "magic" moment while facing the beautiful reverse image of our own best self and our own highest values through a work of art.

It cannot be emphasized enough in today's oversimplified society that art projecting the ideal does not hold a mirror up to a sentimental, sweetened version of everyday life nor does it hold a mirror up to a utopian "idealistic" dream. *Ideal art holds a mirror up to a soul*...the artist's and our own. This is the greatest purpose of serious art: to provide for us that unparalleled moment of heightened self recognition and self experience by providing the physical link that lets us connect with our deepest inner selves. This is the reason we respond to some works of art but not to others. We respond to art created by a soulmate, and by responding, we complete the circle of creation. Music can let us connect with feelings of love and hope and victory...and honorable defeat; painting and sculpture can let us see and feel glorious images of the possible, even of the *perfect,* to let us share in that rare and illusive instant of perfection; fiction and drama can weave for us the stimulating stories of heroic behavior that let us play out in time the experiences of efficacy and achievement; poetry can distill for us the scintillating essence of a priceless moment or observation. The arts can sing to our souls—if they would—and the music of Life is everywhere: in the shapes and sounds and the rhythms and rhymes of words; in the arabesque of sculptural passages edging a bronze or marble nude; in the movement of a real body spinning effortlessly and gracefully through space; in the color harmonies and the sweeping brushstrokes of paint; and in music itself which, at its best, is pure spirit transformed into pure sound.

These are what art could be. What it has been in ages past. What it can be again...but now in *our* own style, in *our* own time, with *our* advanced knowledge and *our* emerging dreams. When a work of art presents us with an ideal vision of a subject that projects an elevated expression of the real world which we know in our daily existence we can, as well as looking inward, look out again at the real world with refreshed eyesight and mindsight. Via the power of such fine art we may experience for the first time or rediscover for the hundredth time those precious aspects of beauty, potential, and perfection residing in the world and within ourselves, which may then act to renew our own perceptions and conceptions and inspire us on to our own personal achievements. Such is the currently forgotten power of the ideal as projected through art.

Few will argue that at present (with some notable exceptions) most artists, sinking far below mere failure in projecting a modern ideal, are seemingly driven to demolish the very concept of the ideal itself. They appear to purposefully dig deeper into the mire, occupying (or preoccupying) themselves with its opposites, the anti-ideal and the anti-hero. It is as if, in the throes of some cooperative tantrum against beauty, nobility and morality, the great majority of contemporary "artists" are determined to glorify distortions of body and soul not as conditions to be surmounted but as monstrosities to be enshrined. Especially in movies and television, where unprecedented technological advancements could so compellingly project human images of both grit and grandeur, those "creating" the mass media appear to bend their efforts almost obsessively toward exploiting their art forms for the sake of sensationalism, violence and vulgarity. Twentieth century art, as the old saying goes, has rutted itself so deeply in the mud that the only thing it can find to clean itself off with is more mud. To compound the problem, the American public has allowed itself to become addicted to novelty, craving ever escalating fixes of shock and horror, mistaking even criminal notoriety for earned celebrity, misidentifying music, movie, TV and sports star idols for ideals, substituting sensationalism for substance, labeling hack misfits as romantic rebels and lauding collectivists as humanitarians.

It is a sad commentary on contemporary Western civilization that more and more people are acquiring "fast food" mentalities and will no longer invest in self-sustaining and inspiring food for the soul: visions of the ideal. Choosing instead to swallow the sensational, cynical, or "politically correct" views of humankind and reality prepackaged by the media, they allow themselves to slump into the indulgent posture of evading the judgment and effort required to select any value system that might guide them onto individual paths toward personally projected goals. These first evasions of mental laziness—suspension of judgment and effort—then require protection in the form of the (usually subconscious) construction of invisible psychological barriers to block any unguarded glimpses of the painstaking but ultimately rewarding self-forged paths toward self-achieved happiness. In the absence of consciously chosen values which would open paths to self actualization, these phantom blockades built to seal off all paths to the possible are commonly (and tragically) patched together from the crumbled ruins of abandoned youthful dreams (ideals) because the "adult" has become erroneously yet completely convinced that ideals are neither possible nor practical. Consequently, even a momentary glimmer of the possible becomes a painful rather than a joyous experience because any reminders of the hopeful child who once believed in ideals have become occasions for mourning.

Far from achieving adulthood, most of these spiritually starved people become "old" boys and girls who, by arresting the development of their interior lives, are consigned to spend their days endlessly distracting themselves by fashioning their attire and lifestyles after the latest "pop" model rather than attempting to achieve the unique and unrepeatable "ideal" within themselves. Others choose a different but equally distracting route of self abdication that consists of spouting political or environmental or philosophical polemics——some of which are even true——without the faintest notion that a deep, useful understanding of their professed beliefs could be achieved only via the personal effort of independent intellectual enquiry or direct experience, neither of which they are prepared to pursue. Mass media "art" consisting of action/distraction sit-coms, simplistic talk show blithering, and newscasts that recast actual happenings into accordance with "reporters'" own agendas before viewers have a chance to think through the meaning of events for themselves all work together to encourage the majority of the population toward this pervasive state of mental poverty. With all the press-coverage concern for the physically "homeless" and the financially "needy" in today's world, where are those in the media "concerned" about the greatest of all victims from our cultural crises, the *spiritually homeless* and the *morally needy*?

For those who *are* concerned, serious art—especially ideal art—has an irresistible capacity to break through every psychological barrier, pseudo-intellectual facade, or dull-witted apathy. It can reveal the lie hidden in false art and it can provide the contrast to bad art. Ideal art—especially exalted music and the ideal nude—can make cynics weep. Why? Because art bypasses our conscious convictions and speaks directly to our unconscious premises (values), the stuff of our true soul. If our "persona" and our *person* are united and the same, our emotional reactions to art (and life) will coincide and accurately reflect our intellectual value systems. If not? Well, many people manage to fake life undetected, but a powerful response to art can let us know in a flash which values really make up our true self. If our true self is not our best self, ideal art can lend us the emotional fuel to improve ourselves with new vigor by recapturing discarded dreams or creating new ones. If people have lost their way, it is often because they have lost sight of the possibilities in life and visions of their own best selves.

The elevation or the "heightening" of the real to create the ideal is a very delicate process, however, which is why so much would-be "ideal" art leaves us cold and unmoved. The work must be full of valid philosophical content in order to inspire, true, but this can also be said of an academic treatise. Ideal art does not instruct, it dramatizes. It trembles with the fragility of life while, at the same time, projecting a passion for living. The passion may be restrained or overflowing, but art must breathe with a palpable inner life if it is to cause a spontaneous—and breathless!—emotional reaction on the part of a sympathetic receiver. A profound art experience, which *feels* like one time-stopped emotional explosion, actually occurs like this: We experience in rapid succession, (1)"aesthetic arrest," meaning that the art commands our attention through the artist's skillful manipulation of a chosen form, (2) "content empathy," meaning we instantly recognize and identify with the values inherent in the work; (3) "Yes! This is the way *life* could be!," meaning we emotionally experience the "reality" of the ideal realized and gain further *inspiration* from the "double whammy" integration of the beauty of form and truth of the content combined, (4) "Yes! This is the way life *can* be!," meaning we gain courage to *aspire* to even greater ideals and make them real in our own lives, to continually rise again and again within ourselves to our own highest level of excellence. The recipient of art is an active participant in this experience. An artist can offer the most sublime visions of sights and sounds, but if the receiver has not reached the same level of value achievement, even the most glorious work will fall without impact on the spiritually blind and deaf.

If the current popular forms of "art" are failing so abysmally to offer inspiring experiences to the small portion of the public who are deprived but deserving of meaningful art experiences, so looms even greater our need for images of the ideal from other quieter and more personal forms of art. Happily, even as we speak, fiction, poetry, sculpture and painting are all being created by artists who are proving to be more enlightened. Powerful projections of "the possible" in these selected art forms are already appearing here and there on the cultural horizon, depicting beautiful and positive views of the world and the human condition. Artworks of this persuasion may be the only life-saving antidotes potent enough to counteract the vast majority of those others infected with an advanced culture-crushing case of diseased vision. It is these worthy works that we must champion.

It is not possible to speak of the human ideal as expressed through art, however, without specifically addressing the moral ideal as lived out in life. Since human beings have free will, they must choose—rationally or irrationally, by commission or omission, by selection or accumulation—their values. Value systems lead ineluctably to ethics, which in turn imply moral standards. This is precisely why the Greeks, who created the first ideal art, never separated aesthetics and ethics. To them, the human form as art became a metaphor for living values such as proportion, balance, moderation and dignity. The human body became a "holy" temple for the human spirit to the Greeks because they saw the human being unified and *whole*, a complete and integrated form of mind and matter—the supreme example of both physicality and intellection. It is worth remembering that "happiness" to the ancient Greeks was not sporadic pleasure but a sustained inner state of moral satisfaction with one's own character and behavior.

The author John Gardner in his *On Moral Fiction* (Basic Books, Inc. 1978) states:

> ...true art is moral: it seeks to improve life, not debase it.... True art...clarifies life, establishes models of human action, casts nets toward the future, carefully judges our right and wrong directions, celebrates and mourns. It does not rant. It does not sneer or giggle in the face of death.... It designs visions worth trying to make fact. It does not whimper or cower or throw up its hands and bat its lashes. It strikes like lightning, or *is* lightning, whichever...the artist never forces anyone to anything. He merely

> makes his case, the strongest case possible. He
> lights up the darkness...protects his...values...and
> all humanity without exception...

Interestingly, concurring with our previously assessed state of the mass media today, Garner had this to say about television in particular—and this way back in the seventies:

> ...[it] is good (as opposed to pernicious or
> vacuous) only when it has a clear positive moral
> effect, presenting valid models for imitation,
> eternal verities worth keeping in mind, and a
> benevolent vision of the possible which can
> inspire and incite human beings toward virtue,
> toward life affirmation as opposed to des-
> truction or indifference.

About art in general he concludes: "Since bad art has a harmful effect on society, it should never go unchallenged."

If we are to meet today's challenges, renewed visions of the beauties and possibilities in life, plus a *new view* of contemporary men and women at their best are our keenest weapons. As other "artists" bombard us daily with images of destruction and despair, so must we encourage and support artists who provide us with images of inspiration and hope. As individuals and as a people, Americans may never have been in greater need of the *idea* of the ideal than we are here and now. For decades, self-proclaimed artists, academic intelligentsia and social trendsetters have fostered, in the novelist/philosopher Ayn Rand's term, "Our Cultural Deprivation." In a 1966 lecture of the same title delivered at the Ford Hall Forum, (published in *The Objectivist*, 1966 and reprinted in 1990 in the book, *The Voice of Reason*, Meridian/ Dutton Signet, a division of Penguin Books), Rand declares:

> If severe and prolonged enough, the absence of
> a normal, active flow of *value experiences* may

disintegrate and paralyze man's consciousness—
by telling him that no action is possible. The
form in which man experiences the reality of his
values is *pleasure*.... Where—in today's culture—
can a man find any values or any meaningful
pleasure? If [he] holds a rational, or even semi-
rational, view of life, where can he find any
confirmation of it, any inspiring or encouraging
phenomena? A chronic lack of pleasure, of any
enjoyable, rewarding or stimulating experience,
produces a slow, gradual, day-by-day erosion of
man's emotional vitality...

In relating her thesis to art, she continues:

In the decadent eras of history, in the periods
when human hopes and values were collapsing,
there was, as a rule, one realm to which men
could turn for support, to preserve their image
of man, their vision of life's better possibilities,
and their courage. That realm was art.... Today,
the very motive that draws man to art—the quest
for enjoyment—makes him run from it for his
life.... If you wonder what is wrong with people
today, consider the fact that no laboratory
experiment could ever reproduce so thoroughly
a state of value-deprivation.... When a culture
is dedicated to the destruction of values—of *all*
values as such—man's psychological destruction
has to follow.... The exponents of modern
movements do not seek to convert you to their
values—they haven't any—but to destroy *yours*.
Nihilism and destruction are the almost *explicit*
goals of today's trends—and the horror of these
trends move on, unopposed.

Such is the same and, as we have described, worse state

of our culture today. There is, however, a major difference: "these trends" in art no longer continue unopposed. Several organizations such as American Renaissance for the Twenty-first Century (ART) have been founded over the past many years explicitly for the purpose of offering a positive art alternative to the deplorable state described above. The fact remains: *individuals* led us into this quagmire of contemporary anti-art/anti-ideas, and individuals can lead us out. You. I. Each and every one of us. Alone and together. But we must first define the ideals we shall set as our "soul destinations" before we can lead anyone (including ourselves) anywhere. We have thus far touched upon what ideals are, how they work when projected by ideal art, and why we need them in principle *and* in practice. We have examined various aspects of our current cultural deprivation in order to highlight how desperately we need ideals now, ideals especially made tangible to us through art.

At this juncture, we might remind ourselves that to create the ideal in art we must search for it first in life. Since philosophy determines the value choices—the content—of ideals, let us now leave dreaming and *think* about the fundamental values that should constitute our ideals for the twenty-first century. If ideals are embodiments of values and certain values vary between different individuals and different cultures, then what we might term "local" images of the ideal will also vary. It follows, then, that if we are to envision the *summum bonum* of the ideal for the purpose of most effectively communicating to (and inspiring!) *all* people regardless of cultural background or parochial creed, we must create our ideals as rational and life-affirming embodiments of the most universal and timeless values possible.

Obviously, the one common denominator among us is ourselves: we are all individual human beings living in the same natural world. All people can relate directly to their own bodies, their own minds and the physical world around them. All (psychologically healthy) people respond positively to beauty, both natural and man-made. Beginning to end, "human" *is* the measure of all things. All thoughts, all emotions, all comedies, all tragedies, all *everything* can be brought back home to the "irreducible one," the individual self. *Humanism* (a predominant concern for humanness and all things relating to it) is the fundamental commonality of us all, which is why the human nude portraying both the body as perfect geometric form and the mind as perfect reasoning function, both realized fully in the ideal, is thought by many to be one of the highest art forms. The Greeks thought so. Enough to create their gods and goddesses as immortal humans writ large. Enough to interchange gods and heroes without Argos's blinking even one of his hundred eyes. Enough to elevate the human nude from mere subject matter to a whole new art form.

In *The Nude: A Study in Ideal Form* (lectures delivered at the National Gallery of Art in 1953, published in book form in 1956), Kenneth Clark asserts:

> It [Greek art] is fundamentally ideal.... Here for the first time we feel the passionate pleasure in the human body familiar to all readers of Greek literature, for the delicate eagerness with which the sculptor's eye has followed every muscle or watched the skin stretch and relax as it passes over a bone could not have been achieved without a heightened sensuality...and when we consider that this passionate scrutiny of the individual was united to the intellectual need for geometric form, we can estimate what a rare coincidence brought the male nude to perfection.

Thinkers and artists of the European Renaissance carried the idea of humanism and the human ideal even further. *The Western Intellectual Tradition*, J. Bronowski and Bruce Mazlish, 1960 (reprinted, 1986) offer us these extended thoughts:

> Human nature has been believed to follow

intelligible laws, just as physical nature has... Secularization, then, is one facet of that advancing humanism which the Renaissance introduced and to which, in some way, every personage...is a witness. It is not an affront to traditional values, but a desire by the human spirit to examine itself.... In each transformation...men have had before them a single vision: the vision of their own humanity. This above all is what the Renaissance did—to inspire men with a feeling that there is a picture of man, the essential man, to which they themselves aspire.

Now it is our turn. What shall be our proposed ideas of ourselves? Our ideals? Who shall be our new (or renewed) heroes? If the ideal means excellence of potential fulfilled and capacities utilized, then images of the ideal evolve from childhood to adulthood and from adulthood to advanced age. Each stage of the evolving self (for we are forever "becoming") can be beautiful and projected in ideal form. This is why, for example, we need both children's stories and mature novels and why we *all* need heroes and heroines, real or fictional. Ideas and values survive history through our heroic ideals in whatever form they are presented in art or in life. Whatever our chronological age may be, it is the ongoing journey from our individual selves to our chosen ideals—in effect, *the process of individuating our ideals*—that constitutes an achieved life. I have posed the following before: "What *will* the next millennium American heroes look like? The American heroines? What a great challenge to create these images!"

In the end, we each must create our own ideals even in order to respond to those of others. I might personally offer a vision of a female ideal, sovereign and full of her own worth, exercised and educated both, intelligent and independent as a person yet feminine and confident enough to yield as a woman. Or a male ideal with high intelligence and all his inherent strength and self-generated power—not the oily, shallow, iron-pumping macho version of today's stereotype!—yet a man also projecting an inner sensitivity and confidence that protects those less physically strong through cherishing rather than through dominance. I might dramatize such ideals in the forms of a hero and a heroine who seek to connect today's visual arts back to their ancient Greek roots and then attempt to advance and contemporize those great images through a rebirth of philosophical and artistic spirit. I might project music that ideally integrates reason and emotions rather than merely stimulating the senses or presenting audio-mathematics to the mind in an either-or fashion; I might extol music that exalts human achievement and hope, and I might explore music that when evoking pain or defeat does so through the use of melody, harmony and tonality (all of which are inherently positive elements even in a minor mode), thus permeating the most tragic of all musical passages with an underlying beauty and compassion that resonates long in the remembering of it. I might envision a fictional, ideal hero who composes such music. I might envision...many things.

So might you. So should we all, acting upon Hugo's words, "...dream to create the future." But we must not dream idly. We must go forward as active participants to turn our ideals into inspirational destinations that can be sought and achieved in real life. Let us each project the ideal in our own minds, and let us actively reach out to worthy artists and let them know that we are hungry for their visions, too, for visions of life-serving, life-celebrating values honed down to their shining essence and expressed in art forms capable of integrating mind and body and soul. Let us fervently encourage and support art that reveres beauty, loves life and honors humankind so that we, as the beneficiaries of such art, may gasp and stare and find ourselves drawn to compelling visions of values like summer moths are drawn to the magnetic magic of the moonlight. Art can be, if it will, a spiritual light. Let us circle round our ideals with awe and get as close as we can to the grand possibilities that glow so wondrously from the ideological energy source within them—to penetrate that source and absorb from it, as if by emotional osmosis, the power to regenerate our own souls and then soar away, renewed, on our own personal journeys to our ever better selves. Such is the eternal power of the ideal. Such is the reason for our present search.

* When approaching the ideal, "achievable" means achievement in principle, not literal achievement. We do not strive, for example, to look like and "be" a particular goddess or hero; we strive to achieve the essence of the goddess or hero within our own self in our own way.

It is not the critic who counts, nor the man who points out how the strong man stumbles or where the doer of deeds could have done them better. The credit belongs to the man who is actually in the arena, whose face is marred by dust and sweat and blood, who strives valiantly, who errs and comes up short again and again because there is no effort without error and shortcomings, who knows the great devotion, who spends himself in a worthy cause, who at best knows in the end the high achievement of triumph and who, at worst, if he fails while daring greatly, knows his place shall never be with those timid and cold souls who know neither victory nor defeat.

Theodore Roosevelt

The State of the Culture:
Approaching the Year Three Thousand

This speech was originally given in October 1992 at Hillsdale College at the inaugrual art exhibit, "Romantic Realism: Visions of Values," *for the college's new arts building complex, the Sage Center for Fine Arts. It was reprinted in* Vital Speeches of the Day *in May 1993. This speech was the origination of the concept of numbering the year 3000 for the coming millenium.*

What is the state of our culture? As we approach the year three thousand, it is reassessment time. Time to stop time, to identify where we are, who we are, who's responsible for our state, and where we ought to go from here.

Yes. You heard me correctly. "As we approach the year three thousand." But, first things first. What is the *current* state of our culture? By way of a short answer, let me relate a true experience:

A few years ago, while recovering from a tennis injury, I worked out regularly with a personal trainer. At that time, the new broadway musical casually named "Les Miz" had reawakened interest in Victor Hugo's immortal book "Les Miserables" on which the play was based. New Yorkers were reading or re-reading the book with fervor on subways and buses, in doctors' offices and even on exercise bikes. One day at my "very upscale" gym, the woman next to me warmed up on her bike reading a paperback of that great classic novel, which she had propped up on the handlebars. A trainer—in his mid-thirties with a B.S. degree—wandered by and noted her reading material with visible surprise. He stopped short and asked in wonderment, "They made a book of it already?"

So may *we* ask in wonderment, "What is the state of a culture where such a question can be asked by a college graduate?" This not-so-young man obviously didn't know about Victor Hugo, nor about the book's existence, nor about the importance of either one to the history of literature. I wish I could believe that this incident was an isolated example of a simple literacy lapse, but many subsequent (and similar) observations have convinced me that this instance was indeed a microscopic but penetrating glimpse into an ever-expanding black hole of intellectual ignorance that threatens to suck the whole of advanced civilization into its void.

In the political realm, presidents and governors give State of the Union and State of the State speeches where they address diverse issues from the unemployment rate at home to foreign policy abroad. These statesmen—I use the word loosely these days—invariably touch upon cultural issues such as family values, care of the elderly and education of the young. Their approach to every subject is usually from the assumption that all of them, one way or another, fall under the ultimate umbrella of government responsibility. Whether or not that assumption is true is one of the questions to be explored in the long answer to our state of the culture question. If not the government, who is responsible for the quality of our culture?

In an election year, we may well remember that culture and politics (even if both are ailing) are not one in the same. No change of resident in the White House can cure the intellectual, moral, spiritual and artistic crises we are obliged to witness as the twentieth century becomes history. Politicians don't create cultural maladies, they just institutionalize them; as with parents, we must give them neither too much credit nor too much blame for their issue. Politicians do not emerge in a vacuum. The culture in which they mature provides the broad educational environment which nourishes (or starves) their development. And who teaches the politicians? Are the universities responsible for the impoverished state of our culture?

In case you hope my opening true story was a fluke incident, I cite recent others to temper unwarranted optimism. It really is as bad as we suspect. From *The New York Times*, June 21st, 1992:

"...during a recent visit to a [Hollywood film] studio's marketing office, a visitor notices stacks of Cliffs Notes for [the movie] "The Last of the Mohicans." When asked if Samuel Clemens scholars might approve of the adaptation of a Mark Twain novel in the works, the producer of the film replies: "Samuel Clemens? Is he a character in the book?"

Now there are some subtle connections that must be made to "get" this one. We must remember that James Fenimore Cooper wrote "The Last of the Mohicans," that Mark Twain wrote satirically about Fenimore Cooper and that "Mark Twain" was the *nom de plume* of Samuel Clemens. So we might not expect *everyone* to follow the full inside track of that story. But shouldn't we expect a film producer to know the connection between the names Mark Twain and Samuel Clemens or at least know what characters appear in the book that has been adapted to the very film he is producing?

How about this? In *New York Magazine*, only weeks ago, a veteran TV anchorman is reported to lament in his forthcoming book about the declining caliber of TV reporters. He cites as an example the newsbreak that the terrorists who sabotaged the *Achille Lauro* were to be tried in absentia, which caused one reporter to run through the newsroom asking, "Where is Absentia?"

Don't even dream that this cultural malaise is merely literary. I recall for you this past summer's theatre schedule for the annual "Serious Fun" festival at New York's Lincoln Center. A *New York Times* advertising supplement entitled *The Shocking Truth* featured photos of a distorted and threatening demonic male face and a female (or the same devil dressed as a female) in Victorian garb holding a sickle in her hand. Headline performances were "Devil in Drag," which explained the photo, and "Mom/Daughter Duel," described as a mother/daughter duet featuring, "a mom that [sic] shoots [basketball] hoops with her daughter's head" and "a daughter that [sic] eats mom's heart." We pass over the obvious grammatical errors to read of another female performer. *She*, not her act, was described as "a piece of tragic art in herself, reflecting the agony around us in a terrifying image and a drawn-out cathartic scream."

Does personal catharsis belong on a public stage or in a private psychiatrist's office? Do emotional purgings that include graphic dramatizations of unspeakable ugliness, vulgarity and obscenity serve any purpose other than gross shock value for the sake of offense? What are the fundamental differences between art, entertainment and psychology? Serious exploration of these and many other (valid) questions would be legitimate in any culture. Unfortunately, most often we are treated to *exploitation* instead of exploration.

Why? It takes little brain work to bewail the ills of existence or to stamp one's foot at reality; it takes even less imagination to propagandize and promote political agenda through the "media" of art. Whether irony or shock or offense are ever effective (or appropriate) as tools of social criticism is a moot point if they are offered as ends in themselves. To what purpose does one joke about evil or trivialize error if one does not also offer positive, redemptive visions of how to enhance life or encourage humanity toward the better? In the absence of objective standards as to what is or is not art, the cults of the freakish, the subjective, the silly, the "dark," and the horrific are left to rule the day. For many—and this includes critics!—the lines between artists and *con* artists have blurred, blended and vanished.

It is significant that the "acts" presented in this festival of "Serious Fun" were not produced by some experimental college group or some obscure Off Off Broadway company or some self-proclaimed *avant-garde* fringe performance gang. This was *Lincoln Center* in New York City, funded, in part, by your tax dollars through the National Endowment for the Arts. And who was the major private money sponsor of the event? It was the Philip Morris Company, a prominent American corporation. To what extent is big business responsible for the state of the culture?

Perhaps you hope the contemporary scene is healthier outside New York. Have you attended the mass ritual of a Rock or Rap music concert *anywhere* on the planet earth lately? Have you really listened to the fringe of that music? Have you *heard* the lyrics that if not outright violent, sexually degrading, suicidal or bald political/environmental propaganda offer at best a content suited to the psychological development of an eight-year-old? Never forget that what is "fringe" today is commonplace tomorrow.

Do you go to movies to see silicon plumped, celluloid couples courting cynicism, fantasy, sensationalism, terror, disease and even death in place of love and romance? Do you watch much TV where "political correctness" takes on mainstream proportions as it is mainlined into millions of brains via media narcotics called sit-coms and soap operas? How about sitting down to absorb the sensational fare dished up on MTV where males and females often defy specie identification altogether? It does no good to sit there and say to yourself that *you* don't watch that stuff. Millions of others do, and they vote and bear children just as well as you do. They also drug out and murder without remorse, playing out in real life scenes drummed into their consciousness every day through the media in a multitude of forms. Understand, I am against censorship of any kind. Totally! But I do ask this: what *moral* responsibility does the media bear for glamorizing the depraved state of our culture?

So. We begin to shed some light on where we are and who's responsible for the present disconcerting, to say the least, state of our culture. We've targeted government, universities, corporations, the arts and the media. But we must be fair. We don't want to leave anybody out.

Well, then. *Who* are we? Who are *you*? Have you been to that sensorial kaleidoscope called a shopping mall lately? Nothing wrong with shopping malls, but have you observed the people *in* them? Have you observed *yourself* anywhere lately? Are you, too, habitually wearing the all-American uniform of a message tee-shirt, jeans and sneakers? Have you asked yourself what you are offering your children as an example of adulthood if they see you listening to, doing and wearing everything you can to imitate *them*?

How many American adults have become merely old boys and girls? Forget kid's lack of courtesy and manners, observe their *parent's* behavior in airports and in restaurants. Whatever happened to parental responsibilities that include not only setting examples for children but also the conscious teaching of values and respect for fellow human beings and even, perhaps, introducing them to the finer things in life like music, art and literature? Listen to thirty-year-old parents announce as a matter of immutable fact that their kids won't read. Won't? Most parents that age are still *bigger* than their kids!

Plenty of forty and fifty-year-old adults are out running every morning; when are *they* reading? What responsibility for our cultural bankruptcy lies with adults who arrest their own development and forfeit the refined joys of maturity by trying to remain adolescents forever? What if we *all* exercised our brains as much as we exercise our bodies? Socrates as well as soccer. In books, not on video. Everyone knows how to play Nintendo; how many know how to play the piano? Do you *know* that, in addition to the perennial baseball trading cards of old, there's a new set of hot selling cards, collected avidly by kids everywhere, that depict mass murderers, sex killers and cannibals? Have your kids—have *you*—been "Bungee" jumping yet? Have you heard enough yet? It *is* as bad as we suspect.

"Culture" in mainstream America has become a brainless sort of psycho-sensory anti-conceptual *zeitgeist* absorbed by most as if by osmosis. It takes real grit to ferret out a breath of hope in the choked atmosphere of twentieth century self pity, self loathing and self indulgence. Our social "air" is polluted far more from the rotting refuse of human values than it is from car emissions. Caught in the tailwind of modernism in the fine arts, "pop" culture right down to the retail business (which has become a form of popular entertainment) continues to invent ever more fantastic versions of the violent, the infantile, the primitive, the mystical and the irrational. And we continue to buy it in every form. At this point, we can add parents and the retail industry to our "responsibility" list, which is getting longer by the minute.

What *about* the responsibility of modernism's legacy? The post, post, post, post modernists—What *does* one call commodities produced by post nihilist artists? "The Ruins," I suppose. Well, that's a pretty fair description of a lot of contemporary art, isn't it? As we know, some of the early European artist-rebels had a just cause in that they were trying to free *art* from the strictures of government control, but many of the original European modernists also proclaimed a serious *cultural* agenda loud and clear, as did their communist counterparts in the political realm. Proponents of both—and many like Picasso were one in the same—knew that the only way to attack Western civilization would be to attack the individual, including an individual's mind. The battle cry in art became *Epater la bourgeois*! ("Shock the Middle Class!"). But in point of fact, what much modernist art tried to shock is the same thing the communists tried to shackle, the independent mind—reason—the faculty for choosing values.

To seek to devalue human judgment by deliberately making ugly, unintelligible, rationally offensive art or to promote contemporary versions of primitive art and political tyranny in a free, science-based world could and still does have only one motive: to destroy the rational values that are the very foundation of advanced civilization. It is no accident that modernism and communism rose and fell together. It should be no surprise that they leave anarchy in their wake.

Instead of a "new world order," we observe, ever increasingly, a new world *disorder*. Why? The answer, I believe, is hiding deep inside our "responsibility" list. Let's expose it now. Have you noticed that each category we have targeted so far is a *group*?

In politics, in art, in entertainment, in academia, the entire globe is splintering into special interest groups as tribal as any throughout history, who seek personal identification (and personal gain) for themselves plus collective treatment from others *as groups* rather than as individuals. America is experiencing—just to name a few!—racial tribalism, nationalistic tribalism, academic "political correctness" tribalism, business "protectionist" tribalism, age tribalism, disability tribalism, gender tribalism, gender *preference* tribalism and countless political and environmental tribalisms as groups seek privilege and power over other groups seeking the same thing. And like their prototypes, modernism in the arts and communism in politics, *all* groups, whatever their current propaganda, still seek privilege and power over the one most important and neglected minority of all: the individual. Now, let's stop to flash a big spotlight on some very shady motives. What's *really* going on here?

Within this increasing babble of "group-speak," we hear more and more stridently the cry to preserve and venerate ethnic traditions: African heritage, North American Indian heritage, Hispanic heritage, and so on. Yet, observe that *Euro-American* heritage has become a dirty word; it is, in fact, the one heritage all the others have come to malign. In a society where free speech has come to mean "politically correct" verbiage, have you noticed how few dare to speak up for Western European and American civilization on any count?

I suggest to you that the reason this one heritage is not venerated (and is actually under attack) is precisely because our Euro-American heritage is *not* ethnic. It is *not* tribal. It is *not* group oriented. It is *individual* oriented. It is *value* oriented. And how are values properly achieved? How but through the use of that other dirty word of the twentieth century: reason.

Individual freedom is still under attack today from power lustful groups. Only the names have been changed to *attract* the innocent. No. Everyone in every group is not guilty of ulterior motives. Many—possibly most—well-meaning people are sincere, albeit misguided. They are what Lenin called "Useful Idiots," followers of a cause who unwittingly further a hidden political agenda by responding to the obvious subject matter of surface rhetoric without suspecting deeper motives. But at the front and center of many special interests groups in America today, collectivists masquerading under the guise of every cause imaginable are still trying to destroy individual independence just as they have for decades. And how better to undercut an individual's self esteem than to undermine or shock or assault or offend or dis-educate his independent *mind* and replace individual thought with "group-think?" How better to control an individual than to shake her confidence in values of any kind let alone values acquired by reason? How better to depress an individual's love of the beautiful and the good than to enshrine the ugly and the bad? Euro-American culture, today, is being maligned because it is *not* a special interest group.

Unlike most "heritages," Western civilization heritage is not physically identifiable. It is not primarily a geographical place nor a genetic bloodline. It is a *state of mind* where brotherhood among individuals is established by nobler criteria than color, creed or collective identification of any stripe. No matter where on earth one was born or from whom, to become heir to Western civilization's ancestry, one need only make a decision to pledge allegiance to humanistic values, the most supreme value being the individual human who possesses the unique faculty of reason which raises our species above all other animals, yes—Dare I say it aloud?— above even the snail darter and the spotted owl.

Nearly *three thousand years ago*, Greek thinkers gave birth to this radical idea that holds (in the words of Protagoras) "Man is the measure of all things." When the ancient Greeks called all others who were not Greek "barbarians," they referred not to the blood that flowed in their veins but the ideas that flowed from their minds. As Isocrates said: "The man who shares our *paideia* is a Greek in a higher sense than he who shares our blood."

Today, we do approach the turn of a new millennium. What better time for philosophical pause? What better hour than this chime of a century to repair to the *source* of our Western heritage to redefine ourselves and begin the work that can lead us out of confusion into another golden era? A mental lifeline has been thrown and climbed from a dark age to a renaissance before. For intellectual sustenance, we need only heed *the* quintessential renaissance man's dictum. Leonardo da Vinci said: "He who has access to the fountain does not go to the waterpot."

That fountain *is* Greek *Paideia*. To help us understand it, let us now seriously view the coming millennium as the year *three* thousand instead of the year two thousand. In order to do that, let's just for a moment stop our calendar to realize how our historical vision has become nearsighted by staring too long at that accepted calendar as if it were the only one.

Don't panic! Radical that some may think I am—You know, I even call myself a "Radical for Beauty!"—I'm not suggesting we throw out the calendar. But I do want to throw us off balance time-wise for a minute by putting our calendar in perspective so we can gain a wider vantage point by opening our minds to the vastness that is the larger human saga. After all, history did not begin with the birth of Jesus of Nazareth.

And don't be too sure about that date anyway. Remember that January 1st became the first day of the year simply because Roman consuls began a one-year term of office on that date, and the first mention of Christmas Day only appears in a Roman calendar dated AD354. Plus the whole notion of the AD system did not come into being until AD525 when a Scythian monk living in Rome by the name of Dionysius Exiguus (known as "Denny the Dwarf") took it upon himself to date the years from Christ's Incarnation.

And even then, the idea was not actually put into use for another 200 years when another monk (in the person of the Venerable Bede) introduced Denny's AD system, augmented by a BC system that extended years backward from the birth of Christ, into England. Remember, too, that the AD/BC method of dating was originally ecclesiastical, and although in some secular use, did not come into general use even in the catholic countries until AD1582 when the Gregorian calender officially replaced the Julian calendar. Most of the protestant states did not adopt the Gregorian calendar until 1700—not *so* long ago. I mean, let's make it real to ourselves that Aristotle did not date his writings, "350BC," "349BC," and so on.

Only in our present "instant coffee" society do we foreshorten our long view of the past by mentally lopping off our cultural links to most of human history. Lately, we further reduce our peripheral vision by "Decaditis" labeling— the "Me" decade, the "Greed" decade—which both oversimplifies and fractures our contemporary time frame into bits of ten years each. In our frenetic race to live life in the NOW we are losing total grasp of past, present *and* future. Such, also, is the state of our culture: Hysterical historical myopia.

So let's pull up *real* short now. Where are we? Like a riderless horse, we have stumbled into an uncultivated field of muck that, we belatedly realize, will become quicksand into which we shall sink after only a few more unguarded steps. Who are we? We are the same as any creature who has lost its way through lack of direction and impaired sight, accidental or self-induced. Who's responsible? *We* threw off our rider; his name was Reason. But now we have removed the blinders restricting our vision and Lo and Behold! we see a stream of pure, sparkling water. Where ought we go from here?

Let us now dip into Leonardo's fountain to refresh our spirit with the Greek *paideia*, the stream of ideas that began to flow nearly three thousand years ago.

Paideia. P-a-i-d-e-i-a. The word translates poorly into modern language because, as with all things Greek, the word encompasses a pulsing, living wholeness of concept that seems foreign to our compartmentalized thinking habits of today. Paideia (*Pie-day'-a*)—I prefer the ancient pronunciation for obvious reasons (it is *pay-dthee'-a* in modern Greek)— means "education" or the "upbringing of children," but only in the broadest definitional sense possible. The operative meaning of the word is philosophical, not anthropological. In no way does it confine its content to a shallow description of societal distinctions such as formal schooling or national characteristics; rather, it embraces the sum of a culture, including "civilization," "tradition," "literature," "art" and "education" in the deepest sense of a multi-faceted but harmonious intellectual environment within which to cultivate the character of human beings in order to approach the potential inherent within each of us.

To achieve this human development, the Greeks broke with the mystical past and sought to discover universal laws of nature, including human nature. They sought to discover fundamental truths about all humans from which they could develop an *ideal* toward which each man and woman, individually, could strive. The genius of the Greek human ideal was that, like nature, it was never static; it was never an unattainable abstract *idea* of perfection but an ideal that, although objective, was plastic (meaning malleable), a living breathing possibility. This is a point often misunderstood by Classicists to this day. The Greek ideal was originally conceived as an eternally "becoming" thing so it could evolve along with actual man.

Through their unprecedented thirst for truth in knowledge the Greeks became the first philosophers. They not only identified man's faculty of reason but went on from that base to fundamentally define man's nature *qua* man, never, in the process, severing man either from nature or from himself. The god/man-mind/body dichotomy does not exist in early Greek thought, nor does it ever exist in their great art. Hence, our true *cultural* heritage began well before the birth of Jesus and even before the birth of Pericles who brought fifth century Athens to its zenith. Scholars officially trace the first of the many great natural philosophers to Thales of Miletos, 7th century BC Ionia in Asia Minor.

But we can go farther back than that birth, too. Homer (dated even earlier to the eighth or ninth century BC) clearly approached the domain of philosophy in his epic poems, especially in *The Iliad* where he displays high concern for the *aretē* in the character of Achilles. *Aretē* in Homer's work evolved to mean the virtuous man as demonstrated both by his warlike valor and his proud and courtly morality— nobility of action and nobility of mind combined. Homer, then, nearly three thousand years ago already embodied an early form of paideia into the *aretē* of his heroes. It is with this poet (again used in the broad, scholastically accepted sense) that we encounter for the first time the notion of an integrated human *hero* united in mind, body and soul who personifies a rational ideal of what man could and ought to be, a universal paradigm for all humankind to approach individually in real life. Ergo: the philosophical genesis of Western civilization. And, incidentally, of a country called America.

The Greek achievement focused on a naturally harmonious world in which individual human rational excellence—not sacrifice to gods or kings, not asceticism from worldly goods, not altruism, not mystical "enlightenment"— is "the way" to achieve personal, cultural and spiritual fulfillment. After Greek expansionism (especially after Aristotle and Alexander the Great) ideological seeds of individualism were scattered into the intellectual and political soil of many nations and religions, both East and West. Wherever reason and individualism were allowed to flower, even if only a little, those countries and creeds were enriched by some measure. But our own Euro-American heritage received directly from the Greeks via Rome and the Renaissance has, on principle, promoted recognition of reason and its resulting respect for individualism.

Some prefer to call this Euro-American legacy "Greco-Roman" or "Judeo-Christian," but what each label basically refers to is the "West at its best": civilized, life-affirming human values identified through the use of reason and resulting in individual liberty. Fully acknowledging rich contributions in a variety of forms from other cultures, it has been the West, primarily, that has actively cultivated and championed individual achievement in all things from right values and personal virtue displayed by men and women in their societal setting to fair play in the sports arena. Western civilization from the Greeks on has also (at its best) hallowed and protected the individual human being's *sovereignty* over body, mind and soul. Political freedom, intellectual freedom and spiritual freedom have marched forward together as the supreme triumvirate forging a common path upon which every individual can proceed to fulfill the possibilities of the ideal and make it a reality.

Today, all of this is in jeopardy.

And finally, *today*, we are poised to target the *ultimate* responsibility for our cultural calamity. *Each one of us* who remains *passive* while others act to return us literally and figuratively to the wild of the jungle *is* absolutely responsible for our present cultural collapse. Governments are made up of individuals, corporations and universities are made up of individuals, the media is made up of individuals, special interest groups are made up of individuals, each parent is an individual, every child is an individual, and every artist is an individual. *Abdication of individual responsibility has caused a failure to preserve and advance the ideals of our great Western intellectual and artistic heritage.* Now, individual *commitment* is required if we are to win the battle to restore to our culture (in contemporary form) those fundamental, life-serving values that enrich a society as a whole by enriching each individual first.

Do not doubt for a minute that there *is* a battle. Whether we acknowledge it or not we are engaged in philosophical warfare, and both our bodies and our souls are at risk. There are those among us *and* those who claim to lead us who absolutely mean to enslave our persons, our property and our minds by *breaking our spirit*. If we are to save ourselves from their tyranny, we must formulate a *positive* program of *ideals* to fight FOR. We must create heroes—philosophical heroes—who sound the call to arms with *ideas*, literally wielding the pen or the brush or the chisel instead of the sword. But intellectual and artistic heroes, like military warriors, are made, not born.

There is still the good and the beautiful among the bad and the ugly, although the former doesn't get as much press coverage as the latter. We are not totally lost—Yet. Through *your* support of beauty and rational values as expressed in the arts, through *your* commitment to individual rights and responsibility (not privilege) in government, through *your* insistence upon corporate integrity from business and through *your* encouragement of responsible individual development by teachers and parents, *you* can—and *we* must together, but WE *as individuals*—begin to create a cultural environment in which men and women today may flourish first *as individuals* in order to become the heroes of tomorrow.

In this election year, a vote for political leaders is important, but it is a short term vote. Let's commit to a long term election for the culture as a whole. Let us get beyond vague bromides that urge us to return to "family values" or "change" for the sake of change. Let us not be satisfied with a hasty re-rigging of the same old traditional ship of state, and conversely, let us also not take a wanton leap of faith into dubious waters of unknown depth without even a life raft of specific description. Let us, instead, chart a well-considered course upon the philosophical stream that still flows steadily from the fountainhead of our own ideological birthplace.

Let us now renew our energies and redirect that ancient stream toward a new high water mark in our own time, in our own place, toward a veritable rebirth of eternal values. The word renaissance means "rebirth," and it specifically refers to a rebirth of the values of antiquity, of Greco-Roman values. But before Rome, was Greece.

There is a wonderful Greek word that expresses the renaissance sentiment even more freshly to our ears. I'll Anglicize it for easy remembering: it is "palin-ge-ne-si'a." *Palin* meaning "again" and *genesia* meaning "genesis" or "beginning." Again the beginning, again the birth, moving back to the beginning but only for the purpose of recapturing the spirit and reshaping the ideas in order to spur us forward toward a timeless yet ever timely ideal. The Greeks defined that ideal. Renaissance Europeans did not repeat the Greek ideal. They reached back to Greece, as we must now do, only to create a true Palingenesia. They redefined the Greek ideal to suit their own needs, to express their own context—David, not Apollo.

Now, it is our turn. Let us begin! Let us not only redefine the ideal again but also *refine* it by breathing new life into an *American ideal* incorporating all we have learned. What *will* the next millennium American hero look like? The American heroine? What a great challenge to create these images! Don't forget that since the last renaissance, we have turned other ancient dreams into reality by flying to outer space and other planets in our adventurous voyage to sail among the stars.

The twentieth century is unsurpassed in scientific achievement. Now we must create a parallel in the humanities by encouraging human beings who, while exploring the "seen" physical universe without, become brave enough to discover an "unseen" moral and spiritual universe within, so we may walk here at home on this planetary spaceship called Earth with the same confident stride that we walk on the moon. No less than probing the inner depths of philosophical space will suffice. No more than an act of Will is necessary to launch us on an inner journey where our final destination is truth. Let reason be our torch and let beauty be our guide on that euphoric inner space walk called "human possibility." I. You. Let us seek the ideal in each of us to achieve the ideal in all of us. Beauty lovers come out of the closet, and lovers of Life come out of the shadows into the sunlight of tomorrow.

It is individual understanding transformed into individual action on each of our parts that must be initiated if we are to drink again from the fountainhead of our youth and climb again that lifeline from despair to glory. If you won't be active, then you are part of the problem not part of the solution. Act how? However you can. Speak up and speak out. Even speaking at a dinner party can shake up some "cheesy" adversary's digestion. Write letters. You would be amazed at how effective personal communication can be: letters to congressmen about NEA grants, letters to corporate presidents (not corporate art consultants) about the art their company is sponsoring which will prevent you from buying their product, letters to newspaper editors, film critics, TV networks and sponsors. Support organizations that support your values—with time if you can, with money if you can. Most of all, champion art that exemplifies your visions of what could and ought to be.

As we approach the beginning of this new millennium—number it however you will—we who love life must dedicate ourselves to those human values that express *the best within us* in order to usher in a future culture that can outshine even the Golden Ages of the past. We must champion the inherent joys of critical observation, of reasoned thinking, of independent judgment, of intellectual ambition, of individual excellence if we are to generate another renaissance of high culture. We must accept the task (and pleasure) of giving attention even to the details of our own everyday living in order to express fully our deepest convictions. We must also communicate to others our vision of a better future if we expect to generate the cooperative energy to make that future come to pass. And we must, above all, create an American Paideia, a nurturing environment in which to teach young people how to think, how to judge, and how to aspire to the heights of their own possibilities.

Obviously, neither you nor I can run around the country explaining to people all the complex thoughts we have explored together here today. But, ladies and gentlemen, we are lucky. We can say, "Look at that sculpture." "Listen to that concerto." "Read that novel."

Art is a shortcut to philosophy. This is why the art that predominates in any given culture can be read as a barometer of that culture's basic philosophical content. All artists are not always conscious of the values they express in their work, but conscious or not, we can be very sure that their deepest, most personally held values *are* revealed in their art, for good or ill. There is no escaping it. Their very souls are revealed. And so, dear friends, are ours when we respond to art. Soulmates are found in art as well as in love.

Art that makes manifest life-serving values can show us our ideals in concrete form. Indeed, art may be the one dynamic powerful enough to *envision* for us a way to a better future. Again we owe homage to the Greeks. They created art forms that could communicate and commemorate the ideals at the center of their great philosophy, forms that advanced during the European Renaissance and may advance farther still if we give them a chance.

The art exhibit to which we are about to adjourn is but a tiny sampling of how well those forms and that philosophy serve us still. It is the same passion for *Life* felt first by the Greek artists that leads these contemporary heirs forward to express a rebirth of values that can elevate their own spirit as well as the spirit of those who experience their art. It is a reverence for and a tenacious love for the beautiful—and for the possible—in the world and in humankind that clears their vision to create images of glory in their art, images that thrill us, that move us, that inspire us. For what cannot be imagined cannot happen.

Artists have always been the dreamers who turn unseen ideas into sights and songs. Whether we follow beautiful dreams or nightmares is up to us. Ugliness and cruelty and tragedy are part of life to be sure, but in *art*, it is life-affirming values that we need to see—to experience—in order to bring those visions of values into existence in the real world. The future is possible because the legacy lives. Those of us who choose it, are that legacy.

What *will* be the state of our culture? It's up to you. And you. And you. And you. And you.

The future *is* possible because the legacy lives.

Whatever you can do or dream you can begin it.
Boldness has genius, power and magic in it.

Goethe

Romantic Realism: Visions of Values

Essay from the catalogue of Romantic Realism: Visions of Values, *an art exhibit that premiered at Grand Central Galleries in New York City in May 1992 on the occasion of their 70th Anniversary and made its Midwest debut at Hillsdale College in Michigan as the inaugural exhibit for the new Sage Center for the Fine Arts building in Oct/Nov 1992; edited version:* Chronicles, *March 1993.*

When we recall the great artists of the nineteenth century, perhaps the vibrant and theatrical images of Delacroix will pass before our mind's eye. Or would scenes of daring and struggle from Hugo flood our memory instead? Or the ebullient audacity of a Schumann song resonate in our ears? Perhaps all three, and more, for theirs was the dramatic, exuberant age of the individual, in life and in art that was "larger than life."

How different are the images of our own generation. Today, in a culture that glorifies violence, vulgarity and ugliness—where art has become bereft of any objective standards—we witness a sad scene as most artists flounder to a graceless finish of the twentieth century. They are not alone. Intellectuals, public officials, and almost everyone else approaches *this* millennial birthday warily. Shall there be cause for celebration—or greater trauma?

The hot ashes of twentieth century collectivism and nihilism still spit and sputter around us, but ashes they are. The 1990s signal not only the end of a turbulent hundred-year era but also the rather swift death of (most of) Communism as a social system and the drawn-out demise of the serious modernist art movement, both of which dominated the period. The future? Some dare to hope, for we are beginning to witness a resurgence of those hallmarks of the nineteenth century: concern for individual freedom in society and a romantic spirit in the arts.

Renewed appropriately, these values could lead us out of

our present morass and beyond, to a veritable renaissance. We hear the word, "renaissance" tossed about carelessly these days simply because we approach a turn of a centennium, but, in fact, the concept holds true currency. Glimmering here and there beneath the debris of twentieth century collapse, sparks of individualism and humanism wait only for a breath of air to flame and fuse them together once more into a phoenix that may rise to lead us, now, into the twenty-first century. If this is to be so, then beauty must be its wings. A restoration of beauty and life-affirming values in art alone cannot forge the path to a full cultural renaissance—only philosophy can do that—but art that makes manifest these values can inspire us by showing us our ideals in concrete form. Indeed, art may be the one dynamic powerful enough to *envision* for us the way to a better future.

A renaissance, however, is not a "revival." The word means "re-birth." We cannot and should not seek to repeat the past. No matter how ground-breaking was ancient Greece or how brilliant the Italian Renaissance or how progressive the Enlightenment, *we* must begin here and now. We must prepare the intellectual soil—in our own land, in our own context—to produce our own unique flowering of the values that made those great periods of history so significant for all time. Which means especially that, in art, a fresh under-standing of romanticism must be advanced and new implications sought that reflect contemporary sensibilities. As "modernism" contrived to put a modern face on primitivism and mysticism, so must romanticism now refresh images of reason and an affirmative view of human life on earth.

We do not plant our seeds in an Enchanted Garden. Like it or not, the present environment is what it is. Art has become a commodity cannibalizing itself daily in order to survive without any fresh source of ideological sustenance. Allegiance to human values, to discipline of technical skills, and to the love of beauty would appear to be the radical art ideas of our time. Contemporary artists of the Romantic Realism persuasion *are* the new "radicals" for they embrace these very premises and express them—each individually—in their work. Philosophically, they (fundamentally) view the world as a positive/beautiful place in which to live and mankind capable of living in it. Psychologically, they view reason and emotion as capable of being in harmony with each other. Artistically, they unify form and content in the same way— and for the same reasons—that they unite reason and emotion. Through examining these premises as expressed in the work of Romantic Realist artists, we may attempt to point the way to definition and understanding.

In a broad swath, we may say that the best contemporary Romantic Realists weave into their work the greatest beauty of nature and the highest thoughts of man; beauty enhances truth, and truth strengthens beauty—weft and warp are tightly entwined. To disassemble this intricate tapestry for the purpose of understanding its construction takes patience. And to further unravel the tangled mess of the present art world in which Romantic Realists find themselves takes nothing less than fortitude.

Let us begin with the term *Romantic Realism*, itself. *Realism* in art may be divided into a wide variety of sub-catagories: "Classical" Realism, "Photo" Realism, "Political" Realism, "Social" realism, the straightforward mimesis of "Realist" Realism, plus a hundred modifiers more. Simply put, all forms of realism in the visual arts present recognizable images representative of objective reality, that is, the physical world, including mankind.

The "realisms" important to our present examination are "Classical" Realism and "Realist" Realism, for to some degree both are employed by the "Romantic" Realist. Artists of both schools produce representational work that relies upon established Western art techniques of painting and sculpture for the physical execution of their art. "Classical" realist artists work within the canons of form derived from Greco-Roman art in order to create the *ideal* through generalization (we are reminded that it was precisely the formulization of Academic Classicism against which the nineteenth century

European romanticists rebelled). "Realist" realist artists use the same technical skills in order to represent *real* life through particularization. We might say that although technically similar, the main difference between Classicists and Realists is that the first seeks perfection and the second seeks accuracy; the first projects universality and the second, specificity.

But the "Romantic" seeks, above all else, expression. Individuality as expressed through the subjective emotions of the artist was—and is—the leitmotif of the romantic spirit. Romanticism has undergone a variety of interpretations. Even such a quintessential romantic as Delacroix, when hailed as the "Victor Hugo of painting," could retort, "Sir, I am a pure classicist!" Nevertheless, one attribute of romanticism is unchanging: a romantic (whether in art or in life) is one who loves emotions. And emotions are highly individual stirrings.

Today, we know much more about emotions than did our nineteenth century counterparts. We understand that emotions flow directly from value stimulation. Whether values are rational or irrational is, here, beside the point; in art we are concerned with their visual manifestation. On value expression in art, the philosopher/novelist Ayn Rand, in her 1969 *Romantic Manifesto*, defines art thus: "Art is a selective re-creation of reality according to an artist's metaphysical value judgments." On emotions, she (elsewhere) states: "Just as the pleasure-pain mechanism of man's body is an automatic indicator of his body's welfare or injury...so the emotional mechanism of man's consciousness is geared to perform the same function...by means of two basic emotions: joy or suffering. Emotions are the automatic results of man's value judgments integrated by his subconscious..."

Needless to say, emotional *conflicts* are the power-packed stuff of which good fiction is made. This is precisely be-cause—as value responses—emotional conflicts are highly charged dramatizations of *value* conflicts. Romantic Realist painters and sculptors, however, tend to project harmony between reason and emotions and the senses. Whether in conflict or harmony, reason and emotions are human attributes, so art that explores these attributes must by definition be anthropocentric; hence, it must be representational and executed through the same technical skills employed by Classical and Realist Realists.

Treatment—and importance—of subject matter can be quite a different matter. Many twentieth century Classical Realists have buried their heads in the sands of time, merely creating over and over again subjects from antiquity through the nineteenth century. Some Realist Realists, bitten by the modernist bug, treat subject only as form in order to address aesthetics exclusively, in which case subject matter doesn't matter at all; the work can be as dehumanized as any abstract work.

Subject alone, however, does not make a work of art romantic; images of girls in white dresses, porch swings and pets are but sentimental attempts at romanticism. For the mature romantic artist, subject matter "matters" because it is selected primarily for its ability to best express the content of a work. "Content" is the pulsing inner life—the deeper theme—of a work of art; it is the sum of the *ideas* held, consciously or unconsciously, by the artist that is revealed by his choices of form, medium and subject right on down to every brushstroke or chisel mark. Content and content alone causes a work of art to transcend its obvious subject matter and communicate, indirectly, the most intimate values of the artist. And it is content, transformed by the artist into a silent melody of visual aesthetics, that echoes through our senses to find an answering "Amen" in the private recesses of our souls when we respond profoundly to a work of art.

But it is, above all, the artist's *feelings* for the ideas he holds about life and about humankind—and about himself—that turn him from a realist into a "romantic" who needs to suffuse his work with the emotional aura of his values. Like his nineteenth century forbearers, today's romantic uses form (the physical presentation) to communicate content (human values) through individual style (emotional expression), thereby making the means and the end merge, blend and re-emerge as one totality of experience that unifies mind, body, and soul. The whole, then, is much greater than the sum of its parts. Herein lies art's ability to afford us a spiritual experience as well as an aesthetic one. The spiritual in art, as in all spiritual experience, is not evoked by an *escape* from reality but by an *embrace* of it—existence and consciousness unified and experienced as one. Remember that one of the root meanings of the word "holy" is *whole*, as in "complete."

With such potent similarities as these, we may wonder if any significant difference arises between our split-by-a-century romantic brethren. It does. It is the difference, in fact, that makes the twentieth century romantic a Romantic *Realist*. Rather than fixing a focus on history, mythology, the remote or the exotic, the contemporary romantic expresses his views through images of the present, of the here and now—the real. Yet once again like his kin, subject matter is handled with the touch of a poet. Images are imbued with beauty and created with tender ferocity or fierce tenderness; it doesn't matter which because it is the artist's temperament, alone, that chooses his style of communication.

Art, however, should be more than just an artist's temperament revealed. There are those who claim that Abstract Expressionists are the offspring of the nineteenth century romantics, engaging in expression for the sake of expression. But, upon reflection, the Romantic Realists are the rightful heirs. Simply to follow the linear path of individual expression begun by the romantics to abstraction is to arrive at the dead end of subjectivity and unintelligibility at its worst or decorative art at its best. The theatre of emotional expression can become the street brawl of emotional explosion if it is not channelled through the discipline of a form versatile enough to act as a strong but plastic conduit.

Another reason that form must be malleable is that ideas change as knowledge and development expand; artists, therefore, must have the continuing ability to adapt form to fresh purpose in order for it to absorb the content of new ideas as well as recast the equally important statement of eternal verities in contemporary terms. The strength of realism as a form derives from its integrative power and its elasticity, both of which enable it to stretch into an infinite variety of shapes in order to contain that power surge which is content electrified by temperament. In his 1863 obituary of Delacroix, Baudelaire wrote that the painter was "passionately in love with passion and coldly determined to seek out the means to express passion in the most visible manner." Once again, we are reminded that form must serve content, even if the content is emotion itself.

Perhaps this respect for established Western forms is what kept nineteenth century romantic masters from crossing over the line into the abstract aesthetic. Some talked about it, and others nearly went over the brink, but the great ones never toppled. Perhaps they grasped that abstract art (as beautiful as some of it may be) is a highly limited art form, one within which they could not expand their aesthetic vocabulary any more than they could fill its shallow vessel with a rich content that would tie it to human life, human concerns and human needs. Within the discipline of architecture, abstraction has ample room to evolve into a complex and noble literature, but in painting and sculpture, the abstract aesthetic must by its nature turn inward upon itself and become an examination of its own form. In abstract art, aesthetics is all.

As for self expression? Demonstrably, it can quickly become self indulgence or else so personal and esoteric a lingua that it holds little interest for anyone other than the artist. Not a few "artists" in the twentieth century have proclaimed a new aesthetic "language" only to obfuscate the fact that they were speaking gibberish. But to expand the breadth of the romantic vocabulary from the nineteenth century romantics *laterally*, within the form of realism, is for contemporary Romantic Realists to meet no boundaries at all. The form is inductive rather than reductive, its potential so infinite that limitless expression and limitless ideas can be explored within the aesthetic, pleasing the senses *and* the mind as well as the heart.

The work of Classical artists engaged in searching for the ideal can become impersonal and codified. That of Realist artists in searching for the "real" can become trivial and literal. That of the best abstract artists stops at the point where all good representational art begins: with a strong abstract design. The work of Romantic Realist artists synthesizes all these various persuasions into a subtle integration that combines their strengths while avoiding their weaknesses. Then, unable to resist—for that is what makes them romantics!—Romantic Realist artists ignite the flame of emotion deep within the interior of their work, and it spreads and glows throughout. If successful, the resulting art offers us tantalizing visions of a *heightened* reality, a reality that is universal yet individual, imagined yet real, timeless yet timely—emotion harnessed by technique, expression evolving from content, and the eternal explored in the temporal: Mood, mystery and metaphor. Possibilities. Passion. Life.

Romantic Realists do not deny and may even dramatize human struggle, suffering or absurdity, but if they choose to explore the underbelly of life, the best of them do so with a higher purpose. It takes little imagination to bewail the ills of existence or to stamp one's artistic foot at reality through irony or retreat into either angst or the endless distraction of novelty; it takes even less imagination to propagandize and promote political agenda through the "media" of art. Artists can address human struggles, to be sure. But rather than resorting to the easy outlets of whine or tantrum, they can express struggle as an act of affirmation, by respecting the power of human sight rather than degrading it and by offering visions of why the struggle is worthwhile so that life might be enhanced and encouraged toward the better.

Self absorbtion and fascination for the "Dark" are pastimes of the idle, the alienated and the angry; artists so preoccupied are serving as the handmaidens of death and destruction. Worse, even, than the nihilism of much modernist art, the deliberate immersion into the horrific and demonic in which too much contemporary art wallows lacks either aesthetics or purpose—except, perhaps, the purpose of shocking an artist's name into headlines for an illusory moment of fame.

Warnings against artistic descent into decadence have come to us repeatedly throughout the ages. Aristotle: "As for those [works of art] that by means of spectacle arouse not fear but only horror, they have nothing in common with tragedy." Mozart: "Violent passion should never be expressed to the point of provoking disgust. Even in a horrible situation, music should never hurt the ears, nor cease to be music." Goethe: "There is an empty spot in the brain, a place, that is, where no object makes an impression, just as the eye too contains a blind spot. If man pays attention to this place, he becomes absorbed in it; he falls into mental illness; he imagines things of another world, which in fact are pure nothings and have neither forms nor boundaries, but cause fear like that of night's empty space and pursue more cruelly than specters anyone who does not tear himself from their grasp."

All of us who love art must heed these warnings. If we fail to generate a Renaissance of the twenty-first century, then surely we shall suffer a Dark Age.

The alternative exists, because the legacy lives.

The rebels, today, are less vocal than their nineteenth century romantic brothers who banded together in camaraderie and with common purpose to become the vanguard; if they are "radicals," then they are radicals for Beauty. Today's *genuine* rebels are men and women—painters, sculptors, composers, writers—who work quietly and individually to create meaningful art from the fountainhead of their personal vision. They care not for bombastics against other persuasions. They work confident in the knowledge that beauty illuminating pro-human ideas speaks through their art to anyone who wishes to see the Light.

It is a passion for life that leads contemporary Romantic Realist artists forward to express a rebirth of values that can elevate their own spirit as well as the spirit of those who experience their art. It is a reverence for and a tenacious love for the beautiful—and for the possible—in the world and in humankind that clears their vision to create images of glory in their art, images that thrill us, that move us, that inspire us. For what cannot be imagined, cannot happen.

Artists have always been the dreamers. Whether we follow beautiful dreams or nightmares is up to us. Ugliness and cruelty and tragedy are part of life, to be sure, but the Romantic Realist knows that in *art*, it is life-serving values that we need to see—to experience—in order to bring those visions of values into existence in the real world. The *avant-garde* artists today may be again the romantic crusaders of the future yet unsung, each armed not with a sword but with a rose.

All civilizations and culture are the results of the creative imagination or artist quality in man. The artist is the man who makes life more interesting or beautiful, more understandable or mysterious, or probably, in the best sense, more wonderful. His trade is to deal with illimitable experience. It is therefore only of importance for the artist to discover whether he be an artist, and it is for society to discover what return it can make to artists.

George Bellows

"The English Patient"
and Other Romantic Illnesses

Published in ART Ideas, *Volume 4, Number 1, Spring 1997 for the purpose of exploring the difference between "Romanticism" and "Romance" in fiction and film.*

O rdinarily we would not give notice to a movie as deeply flawed as "The English Patient." From time to time, however, it can be productive to explore the negative in works of "art" for the purpose of illuminating the positive. With this in mind—especially because of the rapturous fawning-over attention paid to it by the press, plus the nine Oscars given to it by the Academy of Motion Picture Arts and Sciences—"The English Patient" can retrospectively garner our attention too. In other words, the "Patient" is worth examining precisely because it isn't worth examining.

To encapsulate a synopsis of the "story" of this pretentious and sprawling motion picture for those who haven't or won't see it isn't easy: The setting is World War II and backward to 1938. The entire movie alternates between flashback and real time, beginning with a biplane flown by a man, carrying a woman passenger, gunned down by the Germans. The pilot survives but is horribly disfigured by burns, a distressing sight that we viewers must endure throughout an exceedingly long film. Thinking he is English, Allied medics board him onto their convoy, but a nurse, Hana, soon takes him off the truck and ministers to him privately in an abandoned house. In so doing she gives up the work of healing the wounded who might survive in order to give what she perceives to be a dignified death to a man certain to die and about whom she knows nothing. Doomed by the severity of his condition, the patient does eventually expire as expected...but just slowly enough and pain-eased-by-morphine enough to tell his tale to its (and his) end. The English patient is really the self-absorbed Hungarian Count Almasy, who has managed to bring with him from the exploding-in-mid-air plane his copy of Herodotus's *History* that he had carried around and annotated while leading an expedition of European explorers and mapmakers in the Sahara. Two of those in his party *were* English, a man (Charlie) and his beautiful wife (Katherine), the latter with whom the count strikes up an affair. So the story, in essence, is about that past affair of the count and Katherine and how it ended as well as about the nurse now caring for him, while she also takes up with "Kip," an ace Sikh bomb dismantler for the Allied Forces.

Now we may ask: Why did the movie receive nine Academy Awards? Why has it been deemed the buzzword of the nineties, "intelligent"? Why is it labeled "Romantic?" That is to say, why does it purport to be one thing (Romantic) when it is, in fact, another—a mere *Romance*? Why has it been dubbed "the saga of love and loyalty" (*The New York Times*) and "the greatest romantic movie of the decade" (*Romantic Times Magazine*)? Why, when it takes just as much sustained effort to make a bad film as it does a good one, did so many people band together to make this film without even some of them noticing its glaring defects? A bad novel can be written sloppily by one individual—or a painting rendered ineptly by one artist—but because of the enormous amount of cooperative effort and combination of talent, a film takes a whole lot of time, money and commitment by many individuals. The nature of these questions alone indicates that this movie is grandly and consistently symptomatic, on myriad levels, of the moral/spiritual malaise from which our whole culture suffers in epidemic proportions. Yes. "The English Patient" is worth examining.

But not in detail. The following commentary is neither definitive nor exhaustive; it is, rather, some observations that may point the way to a more discriminating viewing of films and novels in general. A plethora of other critical observations have been omitted simply because the chronicling of concrete problems with the film that would be relevant to our larger subject would become a tedious catalogue as boring as the film itself. Let us try, instead, to focus on a few salient particulars that reveal "The English Patient" as a film populated with unsympathetic characters, contriving life neither as it is nor as it could be, and at the same time, suggest some of the criteria to help define what films (or novels) of this alleged type might or should be.

"A saga of love and loyalty?" Well, Katherine is (apparently satisfactorily) married to Charlie when she meets the count on expedition. Charlie is sketchily depicted, but he does have some values going for him in that he is a British spy undercover, so for starters, Katherine is certainly *disloyal* to her husband, whom she seems to love. The count becomes obsessed with Katherine in a bunch of fragmented and meaningless scenes: following her to market, staring silently and incessantly at her, dancing intensely with her, and so on. Katherine becomes fascinated with his obsession and *cannot* resist him sexually.

It is at this juncture where the movie becomes a "romance" story rather than a romantic one. Romance novels and films (sometimes mislabeled "Romantic," especially by critics) are usually based in the Naturalist character and "story"-driven school of writing rather than the Romantic theme and plot-driven school; that is to say an episodic narrative is wound around certain characters (or the other way round) in Naturalism whereas both characters and a purposeful plot are created to dramatize an underlying theme or idea in Romanticism. But unlike what we might term the "regular" or "naturalistic" Naturalism of ordinary people sagas, romance stories are heavily laced with emotionally manipulative pseudo-romanticism in the sense of being set in some exotic place with some so-called exotic or "sexy" characters feeling lots of feelings.

Appealing largely to females, romance stories are usually about relationships rather than ideas, often adventure/love/fantasy stories about women being "swept away" by their emotions and unable to control their irrational desires or actions because of a male attraction or even what they perceive to be a *love* that they can't or don't want to explain. Conversely, Romantic novels and films are about heroes and heroines of high moral stature, offering an opportunity to explore real-life conflicts that resolute individuals may confront and overcome. Suspense in this type of fiction comes from recognition of man's real-life volitional nature transformed into the thrill of experiencing the characters' free will in action.* The adventure of such stories is rooted in the limitless possibilities available to all of us in real life but selectively dramatized in a novel or a film. A "Romantic" love story, then, would by definition deal with values and choices; it would not only show us *what* characters choose but also offer reasons for *why* they choose it. The characters would by necessity (because they are responsible for their thoughts and actions—free will) be philosophically *and* psychologically motivated, and the events of the story would be plotted solely to dramatize a theme. Even if certain characters behave illogically, the narrative would still unfold logically, according to the interaction of the characters, their implicit or explicit values, and their circumstances.

"The English Patient's" major fault—aside from the pure chaos of its disjointed flow of events—is its utter failure to provide motivation for any of the actions taken by virtually all of the characters. If we cannot understand why they act as they do, it is impossible to care about them as people, or about what they do, or about what happens to them when they do it. We never learn why the count is obsessed with stalking Katherine. She is beautiful, seems intelligent, tells good stories around the fire and shops for oriental rugs, but is this enough? Nor, especially of import, are we told why Katherine finds *him* so irresistible that she is drawn against her better instincts into a fanatic sexual relationship with him, jeopardizing her marriage (and eventually killing it, literally) by cuckolding what appears to be a perfectly fine and loving husband. Rather than portraying passion, which is a fierce devotion to values or a valued one, the count and Katherine merely portray raw lust. The count is involved in archaeology, he recites poetry, and he reads and footnotes Herodotus, all of which smacks of intelligence, but since he projects no depth of character he remains frankly a self centered boor, reminding us of the old Rabbinical warning to "beware of donkeys laden with books." And later, he cements our lack of compassion for him by unremorsefully admitting that he directly caused the death of thousands of allied soldiers by trading maps to the Nazis in return for transportation to retrieve Katherine's dead body (no need for her to die, either). Romantic love and loyalty? His unconscionable behavior displays a morbid indifference toward the living, hence to life itself.

The nurse Hana is attracted to Kip because...? He *does* look good with his shirt off, agreed. But is this enough to go to bed with him, even if he marks the path to that bed with candles lit to show the way? This candle scene, incidently, would be magnificently romantic if the characters, instead of just *making* love were actually *in* love for authentic and mature reasons, the latter meaning that they found each other to be the stylistically enchanting embodiments of each other's values. Hana could be attracted to Kip (the only interesting character in the cast) because he is skilled in discovering and disarming bombs and minefields—saving lives—or because he projects seriousness of purpose and efficacy, but we are given no indication that these admirable traits are the ones Hana finds paramount. Kip deserves a better story to be in, but even with this potentially appealing character, we never learn why he is attracted to Hana. She gives him olive oil for his long mane of hair, which is nice, she shows compassion for a dying man who is completely without merit as a human being, and she plays the piano—but the latter is only so Kip can come and save her by finding a hidden bomb in the instrument, only one of the many irritating directorial contrivances to create suspense when the actual story provides none.

All this may titillate those who find *romance* stories compatible with their own erroneous premises about the "chemistry" of love, especially those who view strong feelings and sexual desire as unpredictable appetites that come flashing unbidden out of some mystical space in the indecipherable blue, striking us with love as randomly as lightning hits an unchosen object—and striking, too (so some feel), with as little purposeful aim and leaving us with as little defense against its all consuming power to wipe out will, judgment, and sometimes life.

But even though we may come to understand the problems underlying "The English Patient"—meaning the different ways in which it substitutes "Romance" for "Romantic" and the total lack of character motivation—other nagging questions still remain. We can see how a *romance* audience might love this disorienting film, but why have other, more discerning viewers managed to get caught up with it in spite of the facts that it has no theme, no plot, and no character development? One might try stretching the imagination to hope that the film was meant to be at least another "war is hell" story, but that would be to stretch too far because, in fact, "The English Patient" is less about senselessness of war than it is about the senselessness of love. And why did it win so many awards? Consider the impoverished state of our value starved culture, riddled with blood-and-guts violence and the numbing degradation of sex, gleefully exploited by popular mass media like TV and movies. The public may just be so genuinely hungry for true dignity, beauty, romanticism and intelligence in real life that they will accept practically anything even resembling these things on celluloid or in books. They may not take the empty cliché at face value but make it work for themselves via some unidentified, subconscious method of imbuing their own value rationale into a vacuous work: "the nurse heals because she need to be healed"; "it's a tragic love story amid the tragedies of war"; and so on.

Additionally, critical acclaim (whether valid or not) and nomination for Academy Awards also give certain films a mystique that may hamper the average moviegoer's independent judgment. "The Piano," a self-consciously crafted film with gaping holes in its story line, and "*Il Postino*," a fatuous little work with a malevolent theme, come quickly to mind as comparables. For all the hoopla, the sad fact remains that, except for the cinematography which is lush and beautifully executed, "The English Patient" misses in every conceivable way. As with so much else in our culture, it is another example of technology outshining content. And *this* sad fact is made even sadder because the film was obviously made with great care. It is probable that most of the many individuals involved with the film lavished their very best efforts on it. But in a society short on rational values, what can *be* the best of even those sincere people who try for it unless they swim against the shallow ideological currents of the day? So we are left with the substitution of slick romance for authentic romanticism, unexplained feelings for serious values, passing infatuation for enduring love, style for substance, action for purpose, distraction for depth and lust for passion. And these are just the surface ripples of a deeper philosophical current that rejects reason and responsibility and promotes sensationalism and subjectivism.

It is clear that the director/screen writer, Anthony Minghella, (in close collaboration with the novel's author, Michael Ondaatje, who declared his complete satisfaction with the movie script as being faithful to his own novelistic aims) gave much thought and attention to his tasks. The writing muddle has been limned already and is undoubtedly inherent in the novel, but the direction, alas, was all too uneven and densely bespotted with bromidic scenes. To wit: if there is a couple left on the planet who haven't figured out for themselves that bathing together can be romantic, here is one more out of a dozen other films to offer the idea, but it appears the bathtub *pas de deux* has become such a trite device that the only thing this director could think of to give it a twist was to have her wash his ears. Minghells's overall *intent*, however, of achieving worth through his work is everywhere evident in this failed film. It is possible that the above elements, along with the seductive cinematography, are what inspired members of the Academy to shower it with so many undeserved awards. Think of it! "Ben Hur" got 11, "West Side Story" got 10, and "GiGi" got 9. They were far from perfect movies, all. But they were intelligible and thematically meaningful in that their stories revolved around real value conflicts on one level or another. How far have we slid in our standards that such a well-intended mess as "The English Patient" should join their ranks by becoming the fourth most lauded film in the entire history of the Awards?

The answer is that we have slid far too far in all of our standards of judgment and taste. The antidote for cultural illnesses of this nature is to come forth with constructive criticism of the ailments, to be sure, but it is even more important to offer examples of health for comparison. It is to the latter purpose, or course, that these thoughts are positively dedicated.

*This core identification of the role of volition in serious Romanticism is believed to have been first identified by Ayn Rand in her *Romantic Manifesto*, 1969.

We are what we repeatedly do. Excellence, then, is not an act but a habit.

Aristotle

The Legacy Lives:
Embracing the Year Three Thousand
in Philosophy and Art

From the catalogue for The Legacy Lives: A Celebration of the
World at its Most Beautiful and Man and Woman at Their
Best, *an art exhibit that premiered at Lever House, Park Avenue
and 53rd Street in New York City, on September 23, 1996 along
with a three-week ART Festival of the Arts, featuring poetry,
drama, fiction, dance and music presentations. The exhibit was
again produced as the centerpiece for the Conference for
Constructive Alternatives symposium "Art and the Moral
Imagination" at Hillsdale College in 1997.*

From moon worship to moon walk the path of humankind has been one of uneven progress, yet the relentless
pursuit of it and the levels of progress achieved during certain
stunning periods in history have resulted in the raising of
our species high and far away from its primitive origins.
Often what we consider primitive today was progress in
another day. Sometimes progress regresses into primitivism,
as in the Medieval Era, and then forges ahead again with
revitalized vigor, as in the Renaissance. The art produced
during any epoch—from paleolithic cave drawings to the
Parthenon—is always an accurate philosophical and spiritual
testament to the degree of progress or primitivism of its own
time, to the ideas that informed it. With this in mind, what
have we to say about our own artistic testament today? And
what of tomorrow? As we approach a new millennium it
becomes imperative to pause, survey, and judge our present
context in order to *choose* which set of values and what forms
of art out of our long human saga we shall carry forward as
our cultural legacy into the future. Today, astronauts sail
space as ancient mariners sailed seas. Science will take us
where we want to go but only philosophy can tell us what
ideas to take with us. And only art can let us experience

those ideas, now, in tangible form.

The twentieth century has been one of nihilism, the iconoclastic destruction of nearly every previously cherished value and art form in Western civilization. The result is intellectual and artistic anarchy. But strange as it may seem, this chaos can actually serve us, because it leaves the way out of the ruins open and obstacle-free of ossified preconceptions that might otherwise hinder our judgment. If we are wise, we will turn the devastation to our advantage, and like the phoenix—that mythical bird of great beauty and self-renewing powers, rising up from the ashes of its own funeral pyre—we can fly to the future on unfettered wings.

But where to start? From whence we came, nearly three thousand years ago. Since our calendars pronounce the coming millennium as the year two thousand, we may rightly ask why we should consider it as the year *three* thousand. Because "two thousand" is an arbitrary ecclesiastical date made secular, whereas the fundamental values that comprise Western thought originated nearly 3,000 years ago in the epic poems attributed to Homer, which first approached the domain of the philosophy that was to become the cornerstone of what we know as Western civilization.

That philosophy, rooted in reason and individualism, was limned in Homer's works by stressing the *aretē* of certain characters; *aretē* evolved to mean the virtuous man, not only in his warlike valor but also in his proud and courtly morality, nobility of action and nobility of mind combined. By incorporating this quality into the characters of his heroes, Homer gave the world its first humanistic heroes; they may have been guided (or misguided) by the gods, but they were personally responsible and accountable for their own actions.

Later, beginning with Thales of Miletos (seventh century BC) and other natural philosophers, Greek scholars transformed their own era into a veritable fountainhead of inquiry, a fount to which their intellectual heirs could eternally return for ideological sustenance, a fount that changed the course of history because those innovative thinkers sought to discover—rather than invent—the nature of reality and the nature of man. They began by observing the world and man empirically. But they didn't stop there. They went on, consciously employing logic, to expand their observations into abstract principles, thereby establishing a means of thinking philosophically rather than mythically, conceptually rather than metaphorically. Therefore, let us, with an eye fixed firmly on the future, identify the primary ideological and artistic legacy of what some call our Greco-Roman or Judeo-Christian or Euro-American heritage at its true source: ancient Greece and the first notion of individual excellence, of human achievement and happiness here on earth, of "man at his best."

We have only to look at the sculpture from the apex of that seminal period of Classical Greece to comprehend in an instant the unprecedented phenomenon of man at peace with himself, his body and the physical world in which he lives. Man able to move, able to *act*; man unafraid and unashamed. Here, for the first time in human history, we encounter the combination of mental and physical health brought into perfect balance by a fusion of the real and the ideal, portraying human beauty in all its grandeur. Here we are presented for the first time with consummate images of human sovereignty, yet always in harmony with human nature itself as well as with the natural world. Thus, the great Greeks introduced the unique idea of a physical world and of human beings *qua* human as knowable, of science as a reliable methodology and human nature as a serious study. Here we are introduced conceptually to scientific inquiry not as "technology" devised to solve existential problems of agriculture, architecture, war or navigation but as an interdisciplinary system for the purpose of understanding the universe, the world and man's place in it. Here we find defined for the first time our mental faculty of reason.

Reason. Health. Humanism. Individualism. Beauty. The predominant values of Western civilization.

There is no desire here—nor any need—to romanticize the

Greeks or Greek society. Yes, women were viewed as subordinate, slaves were owned, mystic cults co-existed alongside philosophical growth, and bloody wars were fought over a variety of governmental systems vying with each other for preeminence. Yes, the Golden Age was a tumultuous period. So was the Italian Renaissance. Benvenuto Cellini's autobiography is as much about papal and political intrigue (and street scrapes) as it is about sculpture. Nevertheless, through applications of new knowledge of Greek philosophy—especially Aristotle, though Neoplatonism was well represented—and Roman art, that era became one of a rebirth of humanism (combined imaginatively with Christianity) that produced some of the most ingenious and important art in Western civilization's history. So is our present period tumultuous. The failed aspects of any era are secondary to its positive achievements, *if* the achievements are significant enough to outweigh the failures. Yes, Americans, too, once held slaves, but what is *significant* is that the country split itself to shreds, brother fighting brother, until slavery was abolished. Even more crucial, for all its faults America is the only country whose government was founded on and consciously designed to protect individual liberty.

Politically, America began near the top, but unfortunately, we have followed a downward track toward collectivism for most of the twentieth century. Why? Ultimately for the same reason the nation could not sustain progress in the arts. Eschewing serious philosophy, Americans have traditionally relied on good old common sense in the ethical realm and an insatiable voracity for a quantity of material gratification that deflected them from any development in the spiritual realm, an area where idea-generated art (regardless of the validity of the ideas) would naturally flourish. But common sense is not enough. And at this late date, now that reason has been virtually booted out of the educational system, even common sense has gone by the way, leaving us lost in a void barren of any value system whatsoever to guide our behavior or to help us judge either our materialism-cum-spiritualism or our present, predominant "art." To further complicate matters, by exploiting the value-confusion generated after two World Wars and Vietnam, the promulgators of the "Age of Aquarius" have led us ever deeper into the troubled waters of subjectivism.

Far from being a "New Age" as we stumble uncertainly toward the next millennium, American culture is suffering the throes (hopefully the death throes) of the most irrational primitive beliefs of all now made grotesquely modern. The contemporary artistic enshrinement of the ugly, the frightening, the freakish, the drug-induced, the occult, the hedonistic and the violent remains dominant throughout our entire society. Witness the increasingly hysterical efforts to sensationalize every form of so-called "art," from performance pornography to "music" events, the latter of which have become alarmingly similar to the rites of tribal ritual. This state of affairs is predictable and inevitable in any culture that abandons its value system. Without values that stimulate genuine emotions, individuals are reduced to a perceptual stage of existence and must turn to sensory stimulants to feel anything at all; hence, the escalating need for ever more harsh excitation. Witness, also, the raw sex and violence in movies, which only assist in mobilizing a lazy populace toward continuous nonstop distraction, simultaneously immobilizing their brains.

Add to this primal art scene the forced institutionalization of tribalism through the euphemism of "political correctness" in newspaper "reportage" and TV news, government, corporate and university policies—and even the court system, where justice may give way to tribal sway on any day. Twentieth century tribes of color, creed, gender, gender preference, age, et al. band together too seldomly for the proper purpose of redressing genuine abrogations of individual rights. They seek too often to establish themselves as power centers formed not for the sake of individual survival (such as that which impelled the formation of extended-family tribes in prehistory) but for the clout of political privilege. If the fraud of these last vestiges of twentieth century primitivism in art and politics—and the philosophies that spawned them—does not soon expire on the altar of subjectivism, the doomsayers may well have their way. These modern manifestations of primeval behavior must, of course, at some point self destruct for the same reason that communism as a political system did—because, in the end, they are incompatible with civilized survival.

Fortunately, there are early signs that this demise may come sooner rather than later because the ideas (all being anti-ideas, as in anti-reason, anti-responsibility, anti-technology and anti-values) responsible for inculcating apathy or anger and alienation into our modern world are beginning to show symptoms of having run their course; even the most devoted advocates of a return to the jungle in the humanities cannot run backward at high speed forever. The novelty of the anti-life philosophy that fueled a reincarnation of primitivism in the arts at the dawn of this century is wearing thin, undoubtedly because we are becoming numb to arousal by shock. Still, even though certain religions have attempted to remain a positive moral and ethical force in our society, only a change in philosophy can be broad enough in scope to effectively redirect the arts so that the arts in turn—think of the power of television!—may then encourage meaningful cultural reform.

Because art acts as a shortcut to our most deeply-held premises (whether they be good or bad), it possesses irresistible vitality and puissance. Through an aesthetic process of bypassing our consciously held value system and going straight to the "heart" of our unconsciously held premises, art makes our most deep-seated ideas accessible to us in physical form. If our stated values accurately reflect those in our subconscious, the emotional impact can be one of supreme affirmation. If a mental conflict exists, our emotional responses to art will also be in conflict. Because art *shows* us our abstract ideas, lets us see them, touch them and hear them. Great art is a vision of values that shows us possibilities—as Aristotle said, "a kind of thing that might be." But as ennobling as art can be, so, as we have observed, it can also abet fear, evil, and destruction. Because of the impoverishment of most twentieth century art, there are many among us who have given up hope altogether and claim that we are a culture in irreversible decline. But if we look closely, this, demonstrably, is not true—Yet. And the reason we may know it is not true is because *fundamental* questions are finally being raised. The value of *values*, as such, is being argued. The tiresome haranguing we have heard for decades over the implementation of worn-out conventions is abating. The call for abnegation of all values rings hollow. The futile attempts at impossible syncretism have been revealed as just that. Too many Americans have finally become so drugged, decadent and dependent that those others who do not look to the government to solve all our problems, are finally starting to search for long-term legitimate ways out of the morass. The currency of conversation among thinking people today is not an itemization of what is wrong in our culture but a reflective analysis of *why* it is wrong, a query that if pursued logically, will lead to the creative part of that intellectual equation: What is *right*? What philosophical system can make human life and the culture we live in better? And what kind of art can give us palpable evidence of what that kind of world and those kinds of human beings might be like?

With honest answers to questions such as these we may absolutely halt the otherwise inescapable descent into another Dark Age and stand, instead, on the brink of a new age of humanism, the leitmotif of every genuinely progressive age in history. Why is humanism so important? About the first Renaissance, J. Bronowski and Bruce Mazlish stated the following in *The Western Intellectual Tradition* (Harper & Brothers, 1960; reprinted, Dorset Press, 1986):

Human nature has been believed to follow

intelligible laws, just as physical nature has... Secularization, then, is one facet of that advancing humanism which the Renaissance introduced and to which, in some way, every personage...is witness. It is not an affront to traditional values, but a desire by the human spirit to examine itself.... In each trans-formation...men have had before them a single vision: the vision of their own humanity. This above all is what the Renaissance did—to inspire men with a feeling that there is a picture of man, the essential man, to which they themselves aspire. The Renaissance made ideas a new prime mover which could shape men and their societies, and the men then went on to reshape the ideas. In this historical circulation, one of the most important ideas has been the idea which man has had of himself...

What has been accomplished before can be accomplished again, now, and by the same method: by making "ideas a new prime mover." We hear the word renaissance popping up all over the country, and popping out of our own mouths, too. Well, a renaissance *can* happen. And it *may* happen. But we who would foster a rebirth of life-serving art and ideas must be not only diligent but patient as well. No one can begin a renaissance in the middle; we must start from where we are. We do have models to which we can repair for guidance, however. If we look carefully beneath the ashes of twentieth century burn-out, we can catch a glimmer of the still-glowing embers from those other paradigm eras. It is a small flame but a constant one that, because of the scientific knowledge we now have in our arsenal, may be ignited anew to light the way to a more advanced and exciting epoch than has ever existed before. Those faintly flaming embers are the art and ideas that have preserved the best of our Western heritage. The legacy of an unending search toward the betterment of humankind has survived, and it *is* being revived here and there across the land in sparks of beauty and life-affirming ideas that may forge their combined energy into a blazing torch to illuminate the next millennium.

A fair amount of the art being produced in America right now (although largely ignored by most critics and intellectuals, who lag behind the times) actually confirms this. Driven underground by academics, critics and artists of *avant-garde* art for decades and largely untaught in any of our learning institutions, the crafts of representationalism in painting and sculpture have continued to be taught by a handful of artist/teachers who refused to let their art forms perish. We owe these men and women—now in their seventies and eighties—a debt of gratitude for safeguarding the techniques passed down from Greece through the Italian Renaissance to nineteenth century Europe and then on to them here in America in the early twentieth century. It is their students—now professional artists in their own right—who are presently coming of age to lead the current resurgence of interest in these art forms, which are based in established Western art traditions. Novelists, poets and composers, too, are reaching back to the past for techniques that will help them contemporize the everlasting verities of life with bracing relevance to our own time and place in history.

The crafts of the great arts of Western civilization are surfacing everywhere in America. But what of ideas? Many artists, today, succeed in *capturing* reality, but how many of them create a heightened reality, one that not only brings into sharper focus selected aspects of life through compelling aesthetics but also communicates ideas? Without authentic relevance to the fundamentals of the contemporary human condition, art becomes either decorative or banal. Without ideas informing it, art becomes a pretty pastime without further value. Most artists are not philosophers; they are, rather, more sensitive souls who intuitively incorporate value premises into their work. Great artists, however, whose work reverberates with meaning forever, are fully conscious of the ideas permeating their work; they, in fact, use form and aesthetics for the express purpose of communicating—beautifully—the content of their art. For these superlative artists, nothing is accidental; they select and include in their art only the requisite elements necessary to communicate their themes. Such artists distill the essence of one image or one fleeting moment (or in the case of literature and music, one finite time-experience) for their own sake first; they make it "stand still" so *they* can experience and return at will to the quintessence of that moment for renewal. Then they pass their vision on to us for further contemplation of the beauty and the values inherent in the work. In this regard, great art is a continual source of inspiration; we can revisit it time and again, always discovering something new and something deeper as we, ourselves, develop. Then, as a result of our own self-realization, we may appreciate not only what the work offers on its own but also what it stimulates in us as our minds grasp insights that the artist himself has merely glimpsed, or as we formulate new connections of thought perhaps not even intended by the artist but which, nonetheless, enrich our lives by result of our own creative process. Good art challenges the mind; it makes us *think*.

Art is not for enjoyment alone; it does not exist just to make us "feel good." Great art opens a passage not only to our inner selves but also to the outer world. It implicitly teaches us structure and coherence through its design at the same time it encourages us to "see" both nature and all living things, including ourselves, more perceptively. A landscape painting made of morning light arching into the colors of a rainbow that hovers over an apple-green orchard may guide our vision the next time we tarry in the countryside. A flower painting of scintillating colors and luscious textures can whet our senses to appreciate the fragility and translucent wonder of petals soft, defined and fragrant, not to mention give us pause to consider the transience of all life, including our own. A cityscape can augment our respect for the soaring imagination and technological skills of architects and engineers. A novel can transport us to different places and introduce us to different people, whom we are thrilled to know. A nude of a male or female sculpture can cause us to marvel at the inherent beauty of the human body—the temple of our soul. Great art does far more than bring us pleasure; it can be a seductive tutor in that by emphasizing selected facets of reality for our scrutiny it whispers, "Look. Listen. This is important." By our interaction with great art we hone our own sensibilities to live out the details of life ever more fully. Art, like a person, has a spiritual center where mind and matter are united to become one.

I submit that only by adopting values based in rational humanism can artists begin again an earnest spiral upward toward a cultural growth that will eventually enrich the lives of every person who will look and listen. Ideas: From philosophy to the artists, from artists to the world. Happily, many artists in our country are imbuing their work with values that elevate the spirit by providing reflective content. *Palengenisia* (Greek for a new beginning) is within reach, because the search is on, philosophically and artistically. Such a quest for earthly beauty and life-serving values—and the art it inspires—is still in an embryonic stage in America. But it does exist. An art exhibit subtitled "A Celebration of the World at its Most Beautiful and Man and Woman at Their Best" is part of the proof that it exists.

Let us now shun primitivism in all its forms and contemporize, instead, the nucleus of ancient Greek thought in order to re-energize the helix of progress begun by those noble minds of antiquity. Let us support modern philosophical ideas based on the same premises but brought up-to-date in our present space age. Let us restore the ageless values that engender true progress and the art that concretizes those values in order to usher in what we may term an "Age of Eudaemonia" in philosophy and "Romantic Realism" in the arts. We can narrow those values down to the same five fundamentals mentioned earlier: reason, health, humanism, individualism, and beauty.

1) Reason: our mental faculty of intellection: identifying, evaluating, and integrating information provided by our senses, also including the ability to form concepts from percepts and to employ logic (non-contradictory thought).

2) Health: soundness of body and mind.

3) Humanism: a concentration on human interests, human nature and human culture. Often misunderstood, humanism does *not* mean a religion of self worship, nor does it mean self interest at the forfeit of others or of the planet on which we live. A philosophy based in humanism concerns itself with the secular world of life here on earth—the universals of life common to all human beings regardless of color, creed or personal circumstance. Human beings, like all other living entities, have a *fundamental nature* that is inborn and does not change. Our primary attributes are free will and the ability to reason. It is upon these premises that humanism is based.

4) Individualism: a concept of the individual as a self-determining entity, free to pursue individual happiness through the use of free will and rational means and responsible and accountable for personal thoughts and actions.

5) Beauty: both an identification and an evaluation. As an identification: unity and harmony in variety. A perfection of form through a fulfillment of potential that brings pleasure to our senses. As an evaluation: pleasurable or approving response to the *qualities* of an entity or an idea—"beautiful" meaning that which we judge to be "good." (Both aspects of beauty function together in art, as it is the appeal to our senses that draws us to art in the first place, followed by the personal confirmation or rejection of the value content that either holds that attention rapt for blissful contemplation or sends us running in the opposite direction.)

A steadfast pursuance of these basic values can turn the coming millennium into an "Age of Eudaemonia." The term *Eudaemonia*—from the Greek "good demon or spirit"—was used by Aristotle to describe human happiness as that abiding inner state of contentment achieved by virtue of living a life of reason. In his *Nicomachean Ethics*, interpreted by Friedo Ricken in *Philosophy of the Ancients* (University of Notre Dame Press, 1991), Aristotle's depth of point was concisely this:

> The end or good of human beings lies in the activity that the rational soul [mind] of human beings exercises due to its highest capabilities and in its best condition. Happiness consists, not in having or receiving, but rather in being active. Happiness requires effort. It is a function that human beings must exercise. The higher the exercised capabilities are, the more intense the experience of happiness will be.

"Happiness," then, is not "I *feel* good" but "I feel good because I *am* good," meaning "I am the best *I* can be." Epicurus concurred with Aristotle's moral ideal as the definition of enduring happiness. In addition, by holding the evidence of the senses as the foundation of all knowledge, he also verified concepts as formulations of abstract thought allowing us to universalize percepts and went on to identify emotions as being the criteria of value judgments. Although Epicurus viewed feelings as purely physical reactions to pleasure and pain, his connection of emotions to value judgments opened the door to a further understanding of the psycho-physical phenomena of *emotional* pain or pleasure as being value stimulated. This understanding leads to an explanation of why we respond so intensely to art; by sensorily experiencing our deepest *philosophical* values, we are emotionally "feeling" our intellect.

"Romantic Realism" in art has similarities to but is not synonymous with *Romanticism*. The similarities are to be found in the emotional content of the art: A "romantic" artist charges an artwork with his or her own value system to a higher power, investing the work with a personal passion that, if the values match, mirrors our own and expresses it in such a sensuous, dramatic and poetic way as to magnify our own responses. But Realism *qua* form ties subject matter to real life (even if the subject is a fantasy) because the forms are communicable through the representation of recognizable images; therefore, universal artistic "languages" are established within each art form—note that all art forms except those based in written or spoken language are understandable to all peoples, regardless of background or individual context. Classical elements in realism project universality of beauty and reason. Ideal elements project the fulfilled potential of natural or mental and physical excellence possible at the highest level in the physical world and in real life. Romantic elements exploit the subjective and often rely on the exotic, the historical or foreign settings to provide extra stimulation. While incorporating all of the other combined elements of Classicism (universality), Idealism (potential fulfilled), and the best of Romanticism (subjective passion), Romantic Realist artists reject the Romantic's "call of the wild" and bring their content home by focusing on the here and now without diluting the charismatic spin of personal style and temperament. The balance and integration of all these elements is delicate and difficult to achieve, especially because it requires objective restraint of subjective ardor. Self expression by some Romantics—as certain artists in the nineteenth century, for example, and many of their contemporary offspring—can become too subjective, to the point where the work loses interest for anyone but the artist and those few others who might be interested in that particular artist's psychology. As Eric Newton states in *The Romantic Rebellion*, published in Great Britain by Longmans, Green and Company, Ltd. in 1962:

> Romanticism claims full freedom of individual expression, it asserts that heightened personal emotion alone is worth expressing, that the means of expression must be forged in every case

> to fit that heightened emotion, and that to follow tradition or...what has been done in the past is to destroy the uniqueness of the individual.... Yet despite the romantic protest against the discipline of law we know well enough that without obedience to law and the traditions that enshrine law no human creative act can be intelligible or eloquent. The wildest garden must be designed, or it becomes meaningless because chaotic.... Intelligibility demands intelligence, and however deeply the romantic mistrusts the intellect he is lost if for a single moment he loses touch with it.

This is precisely why great art must be based in ideas. The techniques of established Western art forms (because of their malleability of form and endless vocabulary of aesthetics) are especially suited to communicate ideas. There is great compelling evidence—particularly in the work of certain contemporary writers, painters and sculptors—that through not Romanticism but Romantic *Realism*, where the romantic impulse is grounded in the real here-and-now world of rational possibilities, reason and emotions are being united harmoniously with form and content to create exhilarating, penetrating, idea-based art that could become the most brilliant of any produced in all of history. This persuasion of art is still in its infancy, but it does exist. Technique alone produces cold and sterile work; emotions alone produce psychological purges. Most artists, today, still remain in one camp or the other. But when form (physical presentation) and content (ideas/reason) and personal expression (emotions) are successfully integrated in a work of art, the physical/intellectual/emotional impact is so monumental that we know our souls have been touched, deeply and lastingly.

Which brings us back to our starting point: the benefit to one and all that comes as a result of a striving for human excellence, of human achievement and happiness here on this earth, of "man and (now) *woman* at their best," feeling their best because they have attained a state of eudaemonia as a consequence of their own efforts. Experiencing those values and achievements through the emotionally stirring art of Romantic Realism offers us one of the summits of life experiences. Add to that the human relationships of friendship—both Aristotle and Epicurus made much of the value of friendship—and love (if we can find it), and we will have achieved the highest joys of life.

The efflorescence of these ideas in ancient Greece was not brought forth in full bloom from the head of Zeus. It was a culmination of energy and ideas from many previous cultures and peoples and experiences joining together in a compatible and timely manner so as to generate a pivotal leap forward in human progress. Like the biological link that transformed a particular lineage of primates into humans in prehistoric Africa, ancient Greece experienced a mental crossover from metaphors and myth to concepts and philosophy. The biological and intellectual fundamentals have been established. But the fundamentals of the spiritual realm are very much open to exploration. And art in its highest function provides a spiritual experience, so to probe the elements of art (including the philosophy that informs it) *is* to explore the spiritual realm.

That prodigious challenge clearly falls to us, now. As European culture was the result of the best of Greek intellectual achievement, and the political formation of America was a result of the best of European intellectual achievement, now let us become intellectual producers ourselves in the one realm left to complete the circle of progress. Let the clarion call be sounded. It is our turn to further human progress by *advancing* the ideological progress that the Greeks began nearly three thousand years ago. The whole world is scrambling to share in the material benefits made possible via the Western heritage legacy. Now let us take leadership in the philosophic/artistic arenas and offer an earthly spiritual component to life's exalted experiences as well.

With our base founded firmly in the best of our Western heritage philosophy—rational humanism—plus the great influx of ideas pouring into our country over the past two centuries from people raised in other lands, an abundance of choice surrounds us. Let us move beyond the present cultural wreckage and seize this moment to sift mindfully through our riches and select only the best life-serving ideas to add to that which is infinitely worthy in our already-great legacy. Let us judge the tenets of competing contemporary philosophies according to their internal congruity and their fealty to the following criteria: 1) a rational, humanistic ideology applicable to all individuals at all times under all circumstances and achievable in real life by practical means, and 2) an objective philosophy where the religious of all creeds and the nonreligious, alike, may pursue their own values freely but may not impose them on others, and where people of all colors, backgrounds and beliefs can exist in harmony together by respecting the fundamental "sameness" that we share in common, at the same time tolerating our differences. Such a core philosophy (and the art it generates) is to be found only within the legacy of our great Western heritage, a heritage that is far wider than any geographical spot on the globe; it is a *state of mind* that spans all place and all time because it is consonant with the inherent nature of human beings. The novelist-philosopher Ayn Rand eloquently connected philosophy and art in her 1969 book, *The Romantic Manifesto*. Concluding an essay entitled "Art and Moral Treason," she says: "...art is the fuel and spark-plug of a man's soul; its task is to set a soul on fire and never let it go out. The task of providing that fire with a motor and a direction belongs to philosophy."

Against all odds we must not repeat the past. The genius of the European Renaissance leaders was that they took the fundamentals of Greek philosophy and made them their own: David, not Apollo. It is for us to refine universal truths in light of our own present context and knowledge and to bring consistency to value systems that contain internal contradictions. We have learned so much more about the wonders and workings of the whole universe and of our own nature than our forebearers knew that another momentous leap forward is not just possible, it is probable. Now, in this brilliant scientific age that permits travel to outer space as routine, the time has come to initiate a journey into inner space—the humanities—to discover a deeper, rational understanding of man as a spiritual creature who *needs* access to the profound meanings of life, meaning that is made understandable through philosophy and is in turn made manifest through the arts, especially through the objectively intelligible and emotion-evoking power of Romantic Realism in all its forms. By championing art that promotes beauty and life-affirming values passionately expressed, we champion our own future.

The legacy lives in each of us. In the *best* of each of us. Let us all rise, in Aristotle's words, to our "highest capabilities" in order to achieve first a personal, inner state of eudaemonia. Then let our individual achievements become guidelights, giving others the courage to strive for the same in themselves until we have engendered an Age of Eudaemonia—an Age of Excellence—where future generations may inherit the best we have achieved, as we have chosen to inherit the best bequeathed to us from our own ancestors. It can be done! Any time of crisis such as we are now experiencing is always a time of opportunity as well. Let those of us who comprehend the incalculable worth of our philosophical and artistic Western heritage legacy join together to turn our present opportunity into reality. The time is ripe for it. Let us become the real-life embodiments of those ideas that will connect the ideological genesis writ large in ancient Greece to our own American revelation writ bold tomorrow. Let us embrace the challenge of the new millennium with energy and confidence, knowing that the promise of the future depends on life-affirming ideas put into action today. Let the legacy live.

All passes. Art alone
Enduring stays to us;
The Bust outlasts the throne,—
The Coin, Tiberius.

Henry Austin Dobson

Art as Interactive Experience

First published in ART Ideas *in four parts: Autumn 1995, Winter, Spring and Summer 1996.*

We hear a great deal today, especially in computer talk, about interactive experiences. Internet "conversations," of course, are interactive, as are all forms of conversation, written or oral. But altering or adjusting story plots (or endings) and designing or rearranging graphics with preprogrammed images is more an act of co-creation than interaction. The same can be said for corporate advertising or movie preview "interactive" focus groups where individuals critique or input additional or different ideas to already existing material. Interestingly enough, with all this use, misuse and overuse of the word "interactive," one of the most important and fulfilling forms of interaction is being completely ignored in our culture. That form is art.

Throughout Western history (up until modernism and abstraction) all art has always been a mentally and emotionally interactive experience. In this sense art has served various functions: For a largely illiterate population, art served to teach and remind people the lessons of, for example, the scriptures and ethics of religions. For a shackled population, art served to reinforce the power of monarchies, feudal aristocracies and dictatorships. In a world without photography, art served to preserve historical faces, places and events. In a world ripe for revolution or war, art served to justify the cause and fire the passions of the populace, especially the warriors. In all cases art was for the purpose of communication of ideas, true or false.

Nonobjective art without discernable content is a modern phenomenon, one that expressly denies the function of intelligible communication. (We can be sure that what may appear to us today to be nonobjective prehistoric Western or ancient Eastern art was in its own time full of meaning, as its functions and internal codes were well known to viewers). If the art is beautiful, we can delight in its aesthetics, but it holds no further meaning for us because the possibility of emotional/intellectual interaction is absent. Oddly enough, in its own way *some* modernist or "art for art's sake" art was functional and interactive in the sense that it communicated anti-values that were anti-human, anti-reason and profoundly anti-Western civilization; viewers could *react* to it negatively or positively. Postmodernism's function is the promotion of activist politics for the purpose of power; one *can* react to it if only to hate it. Abstract art that is not merely decorative purports to project a manifestation of an anti- or other-than-material world, form without human content; in spite of the fact that certain artists who made (and make) it professed to be ideological or metaphysically inspired, the art on its own cannot offer an interactive experience because it does not contain objectively-understandable conceptual content; the only "experience" one could have would be sensory, hence perceptual. It may also be worth mentioning that much contemporary *representational* painting and sculpture precludes any interactive experience on the part of the viewer, as well, if it "represents" recognizable reality only as shape or form without any deeper content.

Happily, the focus for our present purpose will remain on content-filled, objective interpretations of reality and the human condition, interpretations that have changed throughout the ages as surely as the world has turned. But even when under the thumb of pope, potentate or pretender and even while swirling tempest-tossed within the volatile storms of social upheaval, the good artist has always managed to present and preserve a very personal view of the world and humankind.

It is at this innermost and intimate level—at the pulsing *value* center of the work—where we find the central, interactive core of the artistic experience. Whatever the subject matter (even when dictated by a patron), the artist's own value system will shine through and affirm or offend our own deepest value system; this *is* the interaction, and we can take from it only what we are capable of bringing to it. By revealing his or her soul, the artist provides us a window through which we may experience our own soul. This interactive experience is the most fundamental, universal and meaningful function of all art because it is an interaction not only between the artist and us but also between us and ourselves. It is, in fact, the only way (other than romantic love/sex) that we can experience our abstract thoughts and values—concepts—directly on a perceptual level. By reaffirming our own values in concrete form, art permits us to connect with the very *identity* of our unique and unrepeatable Self. In order to fulfill this mighty function in painting and sculpture the work must be representational, for only realism in the visual arts has a rich and malleable enough vocabulary of form to be able to communicate profound human content...ideas.

Today, alas, we find ourselves in a predicament. Because of the prevalence of abstract, non-objective and even un-intelligible art in the twentieth century, many people understandably feel insecure about their abilities to decipher, judge and appreciate representational painting and sculpture. This plight must be addressed for the sake of both artist and audience. The following is far from even an introductory guide to the countless aspects that combine to afford us a meaningful experience of art; it is merely a broad identi-fication of categories with some specific examples for the purpose of pointing the way to a deeper exploration into the endeavor (and pleasure) of appreciating the visual arts on all levels. But still, it is a beginning.

The following analyses of three works of sculpture may provide examples of how we might learn to "interact" with any good work of art in order to enrich our experience of it. I have chosen three well-known works from three distinctly different periods of history. To keep the parallels as close as possible, all three figures are male and all three sculptors are male. In addition, both the deceptively simple physical presentation of all three works and the immediately accessible meaning of each can be appreciated by a novice. But as we shall see, every good work of art will capture the imagination of the connoisseur, too, because of its ever-unfolding inner complexities. Here we shall explore and discover both the obvious and more profound fascinations inherent in Michelangelo's *David*, Rodin's *The Thinker* and EvAngelos Frudakis's *The Signer*. Michelangelo, of course, stands at the summit of Renaissance achievement, nineteenth-century Rodin is known as the Father of Modern Sculpture, and Frudakis is assuredly one of the notable living American sculptors of the twentieth century. In the works selected for review, we shall explore the intertwining avenues of subject matter, form and content in order to "interact" with each piece. The success of this interactive process will depend not only on the skill of the sculptor but also on our own value system and the level of our own personal development. Unlike fiction, music, or drama (which are time experiences) the impact of painting and sculpture will likely hit almost everyone instantaneously, so it is important to know at the outset that the subsequent order and arrangement of intellectual and aesthetic appreciation need not be linear. As with all of the fine arts, the depth of experience is ultimately dependent on each individual's psychology and philo-sophical value system.

In light of the last statement, it may surprise some to learn that the first step to approaching any work of art should be nonintellectual. During an initial encounter we must just let ourselves "be." Time enough, later, to judge our responses in the brilliant light of reason. This, incidentally, is one of the reasons to avoid taking guided tours either in person or by tape until the art has already been viewed personally, thereby giving ourselves the unbiased opportunity to respond to it freshly in our own time, in our own way. In the beginning, we must resist prejudging, preconceiving or censoring our reactions and just let ourselves "go." After the flame of first love (or hate) has tempered a bit, *then* we can intellectually identify and evaluate what has already happened to us emotionally in order to further enlighten and enrich our experience.

An exceedingly satisfying, intellectual examination can be divided into three parts. It should be remembered that in any really fine work of painting or sculpture these parts will be integrated so seamlessly—making the whole so much greater than the sum of its parts—that we might feel discomfort or even reluctance when undertaking a thoughtful analysis of it. But the effort will be more than rewarded when, after diligent scrutiny, the work assumes more meaning and offers augmented pleasure. A brief survey of the three components is as follows:

Subject: Subject matter *matters* in representational work because it is selected by an attentive artist as the best vehicle for expression of the deeper content—or theme—of a work of art. The subject should be a concrete manifestation of the ideas contained in the work. As noted earlier, some realists influenced by modernism treat subject only as form in order to address aesthetics exclusively, in which case the work can be as dehumanized as any abstract work. Other would-be romantic realists *substitute* subject matter for content, offering us insipid images such as girls in white dresses, flower-adorned porches, swings and mooning couples on a beach—evoking mere sentimentality rather than value-stimulated emotions. The consummate artist selects subject matter because of its significant power to project a larger theme.

Form (including aesthetics): Since content is crucial in good representational art, the choice and treatment of form—the immediately discernable, physical presentation—should effectively illuminate the content of a piece. Form will determine the fundamental structure and the underlying abstract design, the size and all other basic physical decisions. Once the primary choices have been made, other aesthetic considerations follow. In the case of painting, for example, note the use of color (including value and hue), attenuated or articulated shapes, use of light and shadow, use of line, the application of the physical paint itself, e.g., "invisible" or painterly or expressionistic or other style of brushstrokes, use of palette knife or other instrument, amount of physical paint applied—this examination can go on and on with increasingly detailed interest. When viewing sculpture, note the basic abstract design and determine whether it is closed or open, a factor that will freeze the piece or create movement within it. Let your eye follow the linear passages at will; if the piece is good, the sculptor will subtly direct your vision to stopping points where the content is especially expressive. Observe the surface—smooth or rough?—and use of detail—refined or impressionistic?—both of which offer important signals as to the "atmosphere" of the work. Being three dimensional, sculpture is the most tangible visual art; do you desire to touch a particular work or get closer to it? Whether museum guards will permit this or not, the desire to handle sculpture is a good sign. Sculpture *should* be caressed; it is part of the experience. Always, as with any meaningful work of art, we should open ourselves totally to the reverberating resonance of beauty and let it embrace us in all its forms and guises. We should let the overall visual composition, harmony of proportion and rhythm of line enter us as they will. They are like the music of sunlight. We can absorb beauty as if by mental osmosis and bask in its redemptive powers to renew both body and soul.

Content: This is the burning center and the source of radiating energy inherent in any really important work of art. We must learn to "read" the deeper meanings behind the literal subject matter and apparent aesthetics. This does not mean "make up our own fiction" and impart meanings to a work for which there is no objective evidence offered within the art itself. But philosophical content (if it is there) will transcend (or hover within) both the obvious subject matter and the more subtle cues of form and aesthetics. This is what gives a sense of universality and timelessness to a good work of art. This is why we can go on for a lifetime exploring and appreciating a single work of art as we spend "quality" time with it. We should learn to understand metaphor and explore possible hidden meanings indirectly communicated by both subject matter and aesthetics. A well conceived, well integrated work of art (in any chosen form) can be experienced "intuitively" as a sum. But focusing on the parts of the whole can provide rewards unimagined for the intellect. Then, we can let the work fall back into cohesiveness before our eyes, back into that "first love" recognition and savor it, emotionally, all the more.

DAVID:

By approaching, however briefly and superficially, undoubtedly the most popularly familiar and most-analyzed-

by-scholars male icon in the whole of Western art, I beg not to be judged presumptuous. I have chosen the figure of *David* precisely *because* it is so familiar and well studied. My reasons are twofold: Virtually everyone has viewed this image repeatedly (if only in photo-image form), so I wish to make the point that much can be experienced by conceptually approaching a familiar object with a fresh eye; plus, I wish to encourage an independent approach by every individual regardless of connoisseurship to all works of art regardless of scholarly precedent. An art experience is, after all, a personal one. No matter what anyone else in the world thinks, it is *that* personal interactive experience that matters; because each of us is individual and unique, so each of our experiences in life is individual and unique. The following offering is only one of many valid methods for approaching a work of art, but

David, by Michelangelo

Photo: ART Resource, NY, NY

hopefully, it will establish the desirability of methodology, itself, as a working principle and a satisfying exercise that can enrich the art experience, whatever it may be.

The interaction between artist, art and viewer may begin with any of the three components of a work—form, subject matter, or content—but we shall begin here (for reasons that will become apparent) with

Form:

Without knowing anything else about either subject matter or sculptor, what can we determine from the remarkable form alone? We grasp immediately, as a sum, that this pure white marble figure is a universal and timeless celebration of human reason and efficacy. It is a tribute to maturity even in youth; to courage and commitment in the face of danger; to the conviction of values turning into action; and to confidence in both rightness of purpose and the ability to meet a challenge. Let us look carefully to decipher some of the means by which we come to these conclusions. How may we glean this information *directly* from the physical presentation of the work alone?

The figure is nude, it is male and it is idealized without being *ideal* in the fully classical, mathematically-canonized sense of that meaning, the latter of which indicates that the sculptor is projecting his theme (content) not only as an abstract concept like the Greeks but also as a metaphor for the daily tribulations and triumphs of real men in the real world. The nude figure as an art form (not nakedness as in "without clothing") denotes universality and timelessness by presenting only essentials and by eliminating all details of raiment or time-related accoutrements that would place it in any particular time frame. All males from their evolution into *Homo sapiens* share the same anatomical characteristics and can be so identified in their most basic state; thus, the sculptor is here directing our attention to universal and eternal verities: man *qua* man, from beginning to forever. We see by noting the slenderness of the torso and also by observing that the figure's body has not yet grown in proportion to meet the size of the hands and of the feet that this male is adolescent in age. The naturalness of the hair is another cue that the figure is young; any codified hairstyle often accompanying maturity in many societies is absent. The face is also somewhat soft of jowl and without facial hair (rather than merely clean-shaven), both "boy" signs.

Maturity is also discernable, however, through both the tensile yet relaxed stance of the body. The weight of the body on the right leg is critical as it tilts the pelvis downward from right to left, which causes the thorax to tilt up in the opposite direction in a typical Greek *contrapposto* position. This position signifies an assured serenity, but a serenity enlivened by the impression that the figure has the full ability to move. In addition, the purposeful expression in the eyes, the tense, thoughtfully-furrowed forehead and the nostrils dilated like a young stallion snorting with impatience all cause us to perceive that the restless energy of this youth is being consciously restrained and tempered by the judgment of an adult. Physically and mentally this male youth is in the process of moving beyond boyhood. He is quietly and confidently a young *man* thinking of his timing, assessing his adversary, and preparing for action. There is urgency in his face, implying that immediate action is necessary, which in turn, implies a threat of some sort but no fear. By noting the sling (already "loaded" with a rock the size of a small tangerine) held by the left hand loosely over a shoulder and the right hand clutching the tail end of the sling ready for the rock, we may deduce that a physical event is about to take place. By the simplicity of the weapon we can speculate that it is neither the size nor the power of the weapon that matters but the aim of the man wielding the weapon.

Mental purpose and physical ability are masterfully integrated in this lone figure, signaling to us that mind and matter (consciousness and existence) can become united and whole, which further suggests to us that we are witnessing a spiritually—or morally—charged moment arrested in time.

The sculptor keeps this moment alive in his subject by means of a variety of aesthetic choices, among them his treatment of rhythm, line and mass. The articulated modeling of the still under-developed but hale and sturdy body is not severe (as might be expected in a "might over right" figure), but its inherent rhythm of "life" commands our attention. Because the smooth surface of the thin marble "skin" is stretched tautly over a rippling musculature and a lithe skeletal frame, we are reminded well enough of the inner pulsing and inherent power of the human body, simultaneously registering its fragility and vulnerability. The abstract design of the figure is somewhat open but tightly composed, implying not only movement but also *impending* movement. The sculptor is portraying that potent fleeting interval between thought and action, one of the most power-packed moments in both art and life. The negative space—the shape of the "empty" volume of space surrounding the positive shape of the *David* sculpture itself—is angular which emits additional, spatial energy. The linear passages of the figure actively direct our vision to keep us, the viewer, energized too; no matter where we start, our eyes will trace, with some stops along the way, a compositional path charted by the sculptor.

If we are drawn first to the figure's face (as we *will* be) we can register the full impact of human intention and focus; then—if we choose a linear path—because of the position of the nearest arm angling down, we will notice the sling, a homemade and puny weapon; this is a boy without material wealth, not a gold-coffered and army-backed king, not even a sword-armed warrior. At the elbow, our vision will jump the gap back to the torso only to slip irresistibly down the curvaceous body passage that, when it reaches the toes of the extended foot, will be vaulted over to the other, standing foot and sent up abruptly to the clutched hand (indicating the seriousness of the threat being met), where our visual journey will *stop* in order to register the tension in that hand, the *right* hand which, holding the end of the sling readies itself to swing the weapon in the air above the head to gather momentum and launch the missile at the enemy—one single stone? But we won't linger long on that piercing thought, for the angle of the wrist shifts our eyes quickly back to the outside line of the arm, and the momentum of that shift lifts our gaze on a fast, anticipatory return trip to the magnificent head, the lush hair and the thrilling intensity of the figure's face, his attention still focused fully on his adversary.

The above survey is brief and far from complete. Countless other, more subtle expressions of aesthetic information could be described; for example, we could spend hours reveling in the pure *beauty* of the male body, especially the sensuous shapes of the back and buttocks and the gracefulness of the legs, but look what we have discovered on even this cursory encounter! We don't ever need to know the identity either of the subject portrayed or of the sculptor who created it to know that we have standing here before us a true *hero*. Now, we interact with that information. If our values match those of the sculptor—if we love heroes—this figure will fill us with admiration and hope. It will elevate our spirits. It will lighten the burden of our own individual battles, and our emotions will soar with the bursting certainty of all that is possible in life and in us, galvanizing our personal resolve and inciting us to exhibit and develop the heroic within ourselves. If our values are in opposition to those projected in this heroic figure, we may feel threatened, perhaps ashamed, or more likely, hostile. Instead of love, we may feel hate. Instead of joy, we may feel anger. Instead of a desire to create more and better, we might feel a desire to destroy what already is. As an artist's soul is revealed by his work so is our own soul revealed via our interaction with it. We cannot deny (nor resist) this reaction, for it is automatic—it is emotional. Because art is a physical manifestation of a mental value system, it initially bypasses conscious convictions and goes straight to our subconscious premises. By the art we love (and hate) shall we know our innermost selves.

[Before leaving our concern with form, we must recognize in perennial astonishment that this dynamic composition was carved so dramatically and sensitively out of a single block of marble and that the marble had been previously worked on (cut into) by the sculptor Agostino di Duccio and that the ruined block of stone had lain around neglected for twenty-five years before the consummate skill of Michelangelo transformed it into one of the most enduring masterpieces of all time *and* that Michelangelo was not yet thirty years old when he created it.] Now, let us move on to another interactive experience with this great work of sculpture.

Subject:

By portraying his heroic figure as a highly significant Biblical character facing his first moment of true test and triumph, Michelangelo—without sacrificing universal and timeless qualities—is offering us a more specific and detailed set of values with which we may also interact. As much as the self-possessed nude figure is a testament to the sculptor's abiding interest in humanistic portrayals of individual volition and excellence combined with a philosophical attraction to the universality of Classicism, so his selection of David as a subject testifies to his equally abiding devotion to Christianity. Within this one figure he has fused a clever, complex, yet universally understandable individual man with a just, loyal God. The individual man he portrays is unusual in every way—shepherd, poet, musician, warrior and future king—and the God is ever present in protection of His chosen people. We begin in the book of Samuel when King Saul, being troubled by an evil spirit from the LORD, asks his servants to seek out a man "who is a cunning player on an harp." [All scriptures quoted are from the King James Version of the Bible].

lst Samuel 16: 16-23:

16 Let our lord now command thy servants, which are before thee, to seek out a man, who is a cunning player on an harp: and it shall come to pass, when the evil spirit from God is upon

thee, that he shall play with his hand, and thou shalt be well.

17 And Saul said unto his servants, Provide me now a man that can play well, and bring him to me.

18 Then answered one of the servants, and said, Behold, I have seen a son of Jesse the Bethlehemite, that is cunning in playing, and a mighty valiant man, and a man of war, and prudent in matters, and a comely person, and the LORD is with him.

19 Wherefore Saul sent messengers unto Jesse, and said, Send me David thy son, which is with the sheep.

20 And Jesse took an ass laden with bread, and a bottle of wine, and a kid, and sent them by David his son unto Saul.

21 And David came to Saul, and stood before him: and he loved him greatly; and he became his armourbearer.

22 And Saul sent to Jesse, saying, Let David, I pray thee, stand before me; for he hath found favour in my sight.

23 And it came to pass, when the evil spirit from God was upon Saul, that David took an harp, and played with his hand: so Saul was refreshed, and was well, and the evil spirit departed from him.

Thus do we come to know the shepherd-musician-poet and the writer of psalms in a scene which also subtly sets the stage for us to next meet the same young man as a cunning and courageous warrior in 1st Samuel 17 when "Israel and the Philistines had put the battle in array, army against army."

1st Samuel 17: 22-51

22 And David left his carriage in the hand of the

army, and came and saluted his brethren.

23 And as he talked with them, behold, there came up the champion, the Philistine of Gath, Goliath by name, out of the armies of the Philistines, and spake according to the same words: and David heard them.

24 And all the men of Israel, when they saw the man, fled from him, and were sore afraid.

25 And the men of Israel said, Have ye seen this man that is come up? surely to defy Israel is he come up: and it shall be, that the man who killeth him, the king will enrich him with great riches, and will give him his daughter, and make his father's house free in Israel.

26 And David spake to the men that stood by him, saying, What shall be done to the man that killeth this Philistine, and taketh away the reproach from Israel? for who is this uncircumcised Philistine, that he should defy the armies of the living God?

27 And the people answered him after this manner, saying, So shall it be done to the man that killeth him.

28 And Eliab his eldest brother heard when he spake unto the men; and Eliab's anger was kindled against David, and he said, Why camest thou down hither? and with whom hast thou left those few sheep in the wilderness? I know thy pride, and the naughtiness of thine heart; for thou art come down that thou mightest see the battle.

29 And David said, What have I now done? Is there not a cause?

30 And he turned from him toward another, and spake after the same manner: and the people answered him again after the former manner.

31 And when the words were heard which

David spake, they rehearsed them before Saul: and he sent for him.

32 And David said to Saul, Let no man's heart fail because of him; thy servant will go and fight with this Philistine.

33 And Saul said to David, Thou art not able to go against this Philistine to fight with him: for thou art but a youth, and he a man of war from his youth.

34 And David said unto Saul, Thy servant kept his father's sheep, and there came a lion, and a bear, and took a lamb out of the flock:

35 And I went out after him, and smote him, and delivered it out of his mouth: and when he arose against me, I caught him by his beard, and smote him, and slew him.

36 Thy servant slew both the lion and the bear: and this uncircumcised Philistine shall be as one of them, seeing he hath defied the armies of the living God.

37 David said moreover, The LORD that delivered me out of the paw of the lion, and out of the paw of the bear, he will deliver me out of the hand of this Philistine. And Saul said unto David, Go, and the LORD be with thee.

38 And Saul armed David with his armour, and he put an helmet of brass upon his head; also he armed him with a coat of mail.

39 And David girded his sword upon his armour, and he assayed to go; for he had not proved it. And David said unto Saul, I cannot go with these; for I have not proved them. And David put them off him.

40 And he took his staff in his hand, and chose him five smooth stones out of the brook, and put them in a shepherd's bag which he had, even in a scrip; and his sling was in his hand: and he

drew near to the Philistine.

41   And the Philistine came on and drew near unto David; and the man that bare the shield went before him.

42   And when the Philistine looked about, and saw David, he disdained him: for he was but a youth, and ruddy, and of a fair countenance.

43   And the Philistine said unto David, Am I a dog, that thou comest to me with staves? And the Philistine cursed David by his gods.

44   And the Philistine said to David, Come to me, and I will give thy flesh unto the fowls of the air, and to the beasts of the field.

45   Then said David to the Philistine, Thou comest to me with a sword, and with a spear, and with a shield: but I come to thee in the name of the LORD of hosts, the God of the armies of Israel, whom thou hast defied.

46   This day will the LORD deliver thee into mine hand; and I will smite thee, and take thine head from thee; and I will give the carcases of the host of the Philistines this day unto the fowls of the air, and to the wild beasts of the earth; that all the earth may know that there is a God in Israel.

47   And all this assembly shall know that the LORD saveth not with sword and spear: for the battle is the Lord's, and he will give you into our hands.

48   And it came to pass, when the Philistine arose, and came and drew nigh to meet David, that David hasted, and ran toward the army to meet the Philistine.

49   And David put his hand in his bag, and took thence a stone, and slang it, and smote the Philistine in his forehead, that the stone sunk into his forehead; and he fell upon his face to the earth.

50 So David prevailed over the Philistine with a sling and with a stone, and smote the Philistine, and slew him; but there was no sword in the hand of David.

51 Therefore David ran, and stood upon the Philistine, and took his sword, and drew it out of the sheath thereof, and slew him, and cut off his head therewith.

The Biblical story of David (manifesting always his rightness and leadership) continues, consistently emphasizing keen intellect matched by spiritual harmony, attributes which are amply evident in Michelangelo's sculpted-in-marble youth and which eventually embrace David into the heart of King Saul's son, Jonathan, and into Saul's own household and army. David will marry the daughter of Saul, and upon the death of Saul and Jonathan, he will be confirmed King of Israel, taking more wives and begetting many children, among them Solomon.

Obviously, the saga of David will cause different interactive experiences dependant on the context of each person viewing the sculpted marble figure that Michelangelo imbued with all of the above-cited qualities and accomplishments. The Christian may bring to his experience a profound feeling of worship for the same God that will later, in the New Testament, send His only Son in the form of Jesus Christ to be sacrificed for Man's sins, sins that originate in Genesis itself. The Jew might take David even closer to her bosom as King of Israel. Muslims can be reminded that Muhammad brought the teachings of Biblical prophets to them through the tutelage of his Jewish mother and his extended belief that he, personally, carried forth the work of twenty-odd Biblical personages, including David, Moses, and Jesus. Buddhists, Hindus and atheists, too, can relate to Michelangelo's nude figure as a work of art on a deeper level by knowing David's story, for each will be able to admire the poetry of the Bible as literature and identify with the theme of worldly excellence coming from right actions and spiritual harmony even though they may not believe in any personal God from whom those attributes are derived.

It is highly notable, when considering the subject matter of this figure of *David* that Michelangelo expressed his theme in the most omnipotent terms possible. Unlike most other works that treated the same subject, Michelangelo eschewed all particularization of David's encounter with the enemy Goliath (save the crucial one: the weapon) and focused strictly on the essentials of his larger theme: that man can become one with God and act righteously in all things against all odds. In comparison, for example, Donatello's technically arresting and highly important figure (considered to be the first freestanding nude since antiquity) comes quickly to mind. His portrayal shows an effete *David* wearing an ornately-adorned hat and boots as dramatic flourishes (complete with *Goliath's* sword) and triumphantly laying a foot smugly atop the head of the slain giant—a misleading depiction, if we don't know the Bible, because David returned the sword given to him for battle against the Philistine in favor of his accustomed weapon and only used Goliath's sword to sever the giant's head after killing him with a mere stone. In bold contrast to his contemporaries, Michelangelo resisted *all* direct references to Goliath in his composition, which makes it even more ironic that his marble *David* was colloquially called "The Giant" in its own time in a grand reversal of subject roles. Clearly, Michelangelo meant for us to view his heroic figure metaphorically. The moment he chose so consciously to portray is not that of a *fait accompli* by one particular boy/man but that of one particular *challenge*—representative of all challenges—to be met by one individual, still-emerging man—representative of all men as well as representative of the still-emerging-in-importance city of Florence in hopes of reminding the City fathers to govern their city as fervently, physically and justly as David ruled Israel.

The endlessly observant Giorgio Vasari (a painter and writer contemporary to Michelangelo who wrote so brilliantly on his fellow artists as to be considered the Father of Art History) relates the following story, which not only limns Michelangelo's sense of humor amid all his many and arduous travails but also hints at the pretensions of one of those Town Fathers who had been made Gonflaonier of that city for life, in his insightful work, *The Great Masters*:

> It happened at this time [when the statue was in place but still surrounded by scaffolding until the sculptor could execute the finishing touches and place it solidly in its physical setting] that Piero Soderini, having seen it [*David*] in place, was well pleased with it, but said to Michelangelo, at a moment when he was retouching it in certain parts, that it seemed to him that the nose of the figure was too thick. Michelangelo noticed that the Gonflaonier was beneath the Giant, and that his point of view prevented him from seeing it properly; but in order to satisfy him he climbed upon the staging, which was against the shoulders, and quickly took up a chisel in his left hand, with a little of the marble-dust that lay upon the planks of the staging, and then, beginning to strike lightly with the chisel, let fall the dust little by little, nor changed the nose a whit from what it was before. Then, looking down at the Gonflaonier who stood watching him, he said, "Look at it now." "I like it better," said the Gonflaonier, "you have given it life." And so Michelangelo came down, laughing to himself at having satisfied the lord, for he had the compassion on those who, in order to appear full of knowledge, talk about things of which they know nothing.

Vasari went on to say:

> When it was built up, and all was finished, he [Michelangelo] uncovered it, and it cannot be denied that this work has carried off the palm from all other statues, modern or ancient, Greek or Latin; and may be said that neither the Marforio at Rome, nor the Tiber and the Nile of the Belvedere, nor the Giants of Monte Cavallo, are equal to it in any respect, with such just proportion, beauty and excellence did Michelangelo finish it. For in it may be seen its beautiful contours of legs, with attachments of limbs and slender outlines of flanks that are divine, nor has there ever been a pose so easy, or any grace to equal that in this work, or feet, hands and head so well in accord, one member with another, in harmony, design, and excellence of artistry. And, of truth, whoever has seen this work need not trouble to see any other work executed in sculpture, either in our own or in other times, no matter what craftsman.

But then, Michelangelo was not just a craftsman. He was a profoundly conceptual artist, and the hallmark of any great masterwork of art is that it transcends not only its technical execution but also its local subject matter by expressing universal and eternal truths that can be experienced by a sensitive viewer no matter what the subject of the art or the personal context of the viewer.

We now have come full circle from our opening "sum" of Michelangelo's work, which is apparent to us from form alone. But just think how much richer we are for the extra investment of extended thought in exploring the narrative value and the historicity of the work, let alone a touch of the personal story of Michelangelo, himself, and the significance of this consummate sculptor's work from an art history point-of-view. For we have now confirmed intellectually that form (including all aesthetic choices) and subject matter in all the greatest works of art are selected by an artist to serve

Content:

The philosophical theme underlying Michelangelo's *David* can be appreciated by anyone from any epoch or of any color, creed or circumstance, for it is universally applicable to each and understandable to all. In this one male nude, the artist has expressed a fundamental truth of the human condition. Every man and woman encounters over and over again in real life moments when risks must be met in order to chart a course to the future. Decisions must be made; they may be physical, or moral, or professional, or romantic, or... We all must, by our nature as volitional human beings, experience both the vulnerability and the exhilaration that come from internal and external challenges to our worth and abilities. Our values determine what actions we shall take. Conviction in our values gives us confidence in our actions. Michelangelo's *David*—along with pleasuring us with the beauty of our physical bodies and the achievements possible through our minds in action—offers us more by *showing us the splendor* of the courage we may summon within ourselves to continue our own individual quests.

THE THINKER

Critics, artists and scholars have written seriously about it. Commercial artists have satirized it to advertise everything from political candidates to fountain pens to toilet tissue. Enigmatic as it appears to some, few are uncertain about what they *think* they think about *Le Penseur*; therefore, we are far from alone in interacting with a work of art that has become

Photo: Barrett Randell

The Thinker, by Auguste Rodin

a symbol for human thought itself. But how many of us have really *looked* at it without someone else's opinion or the cliché of the pose leading our vision? For this work (because of its notoriety) we have little choice but to begin our brief examination with

Subject:

Originally conceived by Rodin as the figure of Dante sitting alone and pondering the inferno of his *Comedy*, the male figure was to provide the focal point for the sculptor's *The Gates of Hell* by being placed above the lintel of the bronze doors that were commissioned by the French government to become the portals for a new museum of decorative arts in Paris. Understanding that the overall theme for the doors was obviously inspired by the double impetus of Lorenzo Ghiberti's fifteenth-century bronze Baptistery doors in Florence (proclaimed by Michelangelo fine enough to be "The Gates of Paradise") and Dante's fourteenth-century literary work, we are struck immediately by the paradox that as Dante's *Divine Comedy* begins in hell and ends in paradise, so Rodin's gates began in paradise (Ghiberti's) and end as the entrance to hell. We also know that over a period of time, as he worked on the studies for his "Gates," the sculptor changed his mind as well as his image until, in the end, he detached it from its architectural setting altogether and turned it into a separate monument with the title, *The Thinker; The Poet, fragment of a door*. The official title was eventually simplified into *The Thinker* by critics and the public both.

In *The Sculpture of Auguste Rodin*, author John Tancock quotes Rodin directly from a letter the artist wrote to the critic Marcel Adam, where he revealed the metamorphosis of his figure from a depiction of Dante into a more generalized image:

> The Thinker has a story. In the days long gone
> by, I conceived the idea of "The Gates of Hell."
> Before the door, seated on a rock, Dante, thinking

of the plan of his poem. Behind him, Ugolino, Francesca, Paolo, all the characters of *The Divine Comedy*. This project was not realized. [*The Gates of Hell* were begun in 1880, never finished, and cast only after Rodin's death.] Thin, ascetic, Dante separated from the whole would have been without meaning. Guided by my first inspiration I conceived another thinker, a naked man, seated upon a rock, his feet drawn under him, his fist against his teeth, he dreams. The fertile thought slowly elaborates itself within his brain. He is no longer dreamer, he is creator.

Whether or not Rodin's final image expresses the artist's stated intentions for his figure to be an image of a "creator" is a provocative question. And what if, instead of *The Thinker*, the sculpture would have gained another popular title that did not characterize its theme so generically? For example, what would its future have been if it been referred to as *The Poet*? It is a fact that although the piece received mixed reviews from critics and artists both in Rodin's day and later, it has been popular with the public from the moment of its first exhibition in Paris in 1889, a fact augmented by the large number of subscribers who joined together to finance an enlarged version to be presented to the city of Paris in 1904, and further confirmed by the thousands of small, commercial copies adorning the desks of countless "thinking" people, today. But why? With these inquiries in mind, let us now turn for more information to

Form:

At first glance—and this may be a significant factor in terms of *The Thinker's* popularity—the figure appears to be depicted in the most conventional of "thinking" positions. Sitting contemplatively with his chin resting on one hand, apparently lost in thought, the composition is so stereotypical of the thinking man that it is practically a caricature. But let us look closely with a fresh eye:

The abstract design is a closed form, freezing the male figure into immobility; whatever he is thinking, he is not going to act on it soon. The next thing we notice is that far from actually *being* the conventional thinking position, the pose is an intentional distortion of it. Ordinarily, the elbow of the hand upon which the chin rests would anchor itself on the same knee (or thigh, in this case) as the arm, i.e., the right elbow on the right knee. But here the pose is twisted so that the elbow crosses the body and leans on the *left* thigh in what in reality would be a very uncomfortable position, hardly conducive to thought. Also, the treatment of *contrapposto*, here, almost schemes to prevent movement rather than permit it. Critics and scholars point to various other works of influence evident in Rodin's depiction, among them Michelangelo's seated figure in the Tomb of Lorenzo dé Medici in Florence, the [Greek] *Belvedere Torso*, Hugo's view of his own person as *Penseur*, Baudelaire's writings and, of course, Dante's. Opinions vary, but the general consensus finds the piece derivative of (or at least to some degree motivated by) other art, whether sculptural or literary.

To this observer (I am not original here; it is apparent to many), the telling influence locates itself in the sculpture's contorted composition. It is eerily close to an étude for *Ugolino* by Jean-Baptiste Carpeaux (a bronze cast of which Rodin had in his studio and is available to be viewed today in the Museé Rodin in Paris). There can be little doubt that Rodin was deeply—perhaps metaphysically—influenced by that configuration, possibly while still conceiving his figure as Dante imagining the horrific scenes of his poem. But in the Carpeaux maquette, the agonized subject balances his left arm significantly on one of his children, and both hands are placed in or near the mouth of a father contemplating the act of devouring his own offspring. We readily understand the contorted body of Ugolino as the outward manifestation of an internal war. But why did Rodin echo that agony in his *Thinker*? Could it be that on some level he equated the agony of thinking the unthinkable with the act of thinking itself?

We notice that the hands and the feet of the Rodin's *Thinker* appear overly large, but unlike Michelangelo's *David* this is clearly not a portrayal of youth in the process of physical development; the hands are gnarled, and the feet clutch the stone beneath them reminiscent of, if anything, those of a late primate or, perhaps, an early hominid. The linear passages of the figure are largely broken (as is the negative space design) forcing our eye into a rhythmically uneven, visually restless pattern that jerks our attention from here to there, from knobby knee to jutting shoulder, over a powerful body that is muscular with physical strength but projects little grace in its bearing. Every sinew of the body is strained as if to physically complement the severe tension of mental exertion, a hallmark of many of Rodin's bronze pieces and a combination that many viewers find sensual. Only the left hand hanging in an awkwardly relaxed manner and one long passage of line (when viewed from the right side) from the top of the smooth, helmet-haired head down the center of the back, curving around the buttocks and continuing along a thigh and a calf, and then releasing into space from the toes of the right foot, provide relief from an otherwise compressed turbulence. Note that if we follow that one unbroken passage, we are *not* directed back to the figure by line; after having our visual path released downward into space, we must come back to the piece on our own, however and wherever. Internal dynamics of modeling are present to provide "life" to the figure to be sure, but actual movement within the form is more a result of crafting a technically-constructed "pose" than one of creating a natural human position.

Anatomically Rodin consciously distorted the human body to suit his own ends, and aesthetically, he just as purposefully challenged many artistic "rules"—both of which caused modernists to claim him as their own. But it must be acknowledged that, unlike so many of his followers, he *knew* both anatomy and aesthetic standards; therefore, his intentional discarding of them acts to instill a certain kind of commanding, decisive power into the work. Regarding surface concerns, in stark contrast to *David's* thin sheath of smooth and supple skin, *The Thinker's* flesh bulges up from the pressure of knotty concentrations of crude muscle mass, yet hangs loose around a collapsed stomach; the texture of the sculpture's exteriors are rough and bumpy and coarse. This is the body of a brute. And the brain of...what? The low frontal cranial plane and the flattened nose again call to mind primal associations. The facial expression, far from being thoughtful—or at least far from finding any pleasure in thought—looks constipated, as if the effort were torture or, rather, as if the effort were being put forth but the mind incapable of understanding. The eyes are unfocused, suggesting labored brooding rather than alert attention. What, then, if we assess only the physical presentation of form might we gather is Rodin's

Content:

This sculptor did not compose carelessly nor did he lack the skills to project exactly what he wanted to; he was a master at expressing content through form. If we are aware of the original subject matter and the story behind *The Gates of Hell*, we might speculate that contemplation of Dante's inferno could certainly cause consternation such as that projected in this robust male. But that would be ignoring all of the other, well-integrated cues of form (for example, the figure is nude, implying universality and timelessness) that indicate Rodin truly did not intend to particularize his final, finished figure nor its circumstance. It would also entail disbelieving the sculptor's own written declaration that the figure had moved beyond Dante's hell to a generalized image. So we must accept this figure as Rodin's projection of the process of *thinking*. Furthermore, we must remember that Rodin, himself, described his "thinker" as "creator." Based on the artist's statement, what implications can we conjecture it might mean concerning Rodin's personal, internal experience of the creation of his own art in accordance with his larger worldview of life and man's place in it? For Rodin, this *is* the human condition, what thinking man looks like—what a *creator* looks like. The more poetic of us might imagine an allusion buried obscurely in the piece that hints at man's evolutionary "missing link," which if confirmed, could render the work heroic by commemorating that arduous and baffling, yet monumentally brave moment in human history when *Homo erectus* struggled valiantly to become *Homo sapien*, pushing the envelope of his mental powers to the extreme and "creating" himself into a higher form of humanity.

But since there is no objective evidence for such a flight of imagination, visual or written, how *do* we interact with this work of art? It's title and at-first-glance pose imply certain positive stimuli: thinking, reasoning man. But the internal and external contortions imply the opposite: painful or uncomfortable mental toil. One could almost wonder if the sculptor deliberately and perversely implanted such obvious contradictions in this work for the very purpose of foiling us, its viewers. Whatever hypotheses we may venture, however, one thing is certain: Rodin's *Thinker* absolutely expresses stressed exertion in every way. For those of us who find intellection a joyous, thrilling, exciting challenge—we who love to think—this image will probably not provide agreeable contemplation, for the strained mental and physical state is not one we experience in our own lives when it comes to tackling problems. If one holds reason as a value but finds the use of it difficult, a poignant yet sympathetic interaction relating to the eternal effort employed by Rodin's figure could occur. If one despises reason and flees from its use, the figure might be perceived as being permanently "stumped," meaning that answers to questions aren't *possible*, a metaphysical condition that would resonate in some viewers with the shock of resignation. Each of our responses to this work of art will depend ultimately on our views of the thinking process itself, as well as on our premises concerning our own human faculties, including their potential, inherent in all humans *qua* human.

We could go on to describe in detail other, ancillary interactive processes that might take place as we accept or reject a value system that would cause Rodin to create this image of contemplation for *our* contemplation. But rather than continue down that avenue of psychological rather than artistic analysis, perhaps we should just look back at the *David*, a figure fully engaged but energetic, and then again at *The Thinker*, a figure struggling but not succeeding—both images of man thinking—and come to our own separate conclusions. Hopefully, by observing both male nudes attentively, we can learn not only more about how to "look" at art but also how to learn more about ourselves through our interaction with it.

At this juncture we have explored, albeit briefly, important sculpture pieces from Renaissance Italy and nineteenth-century France. To approach one of the most significant works of twentieth-century America, we shall now turn to a national monument by EvAngelos Frudakis:

THE SIGNER

To stand before this great work of art is to confront—and embrace, if our value system will warrant it—the entire concept of human sovereignty and individual freedom, not just politically but morally and spiritually, presented to us in one solitary figure. Because we began our analyses with form in considering *David* and subject matter when addressing *The Thinker*, let us here begin our survey with

The Signer, by EvAngelos Frudakis

Content:

Even looking at a photograph of *The Signer* without ever viewing or knowing the location of the physical monument, Plutarch's words (from *On the Fortune or Virtue of Alexander*) may come unbidden to mind: "For Lysippus [a Greek master sculptor of antiquity] was, it seemed, the only one that revealed in the bronze Alexander character and in molding his form portrayed also his virtues...." Just so can we readily perceive Frudakis's artistic achievement. [Immaterial to the point but, by happy coincidence, EvAngelos Frudakis is an American of Greek heritage.] Immediately upon a first glance we can grasp the content of *The Signer* as a portrayal of an intellectual hero. He holds a pen in one hand and exultantly thrusts rolled paper documents into the air with the other, the triumphant expression on his face and the rippling muscles of his physique declaring the power and conviction of mind and body united in one moment of supreme fulfillment. The composition of the piece in every way proclaims both aesthetic and ethical harmony. The period clothing informs us that this male figure is not contemporary, but his inner spirit assures us that he is symbolic of what is possible to all humankind for all time. By the pen and paper we know he is a thinker who acts confidently on his judgement and succeeds brilliantly in his endeavors. This is not a mere scribe. This is a producer. *David* with his sling and determination is a heroic defender of the faith; *The Thinker* with his contorted body and stumped expression is a paralyzed boor; *The Signer* in his stance at his grand moment of efficacy is an originator, a self-generated "doer."

Let us abate our curiosity concerning the subject's identity by postponing knowledge of subject matter, which may or may not (depending on the skill and intent of the artist) confirm our first impressions of content, by looking next to

Form:

The overall abstract design of this piece is teeming with movement, excitement, and power. Even the negative volumes of space are made up of angles and relieved only by long sweeps of linear passages, the first of which causes our eyes to slide from the papers held aloft down the outer edge of the raised arm along the tautly-arched body to the weight-bearing foot. At this point there is no pause as our vision is vaulted swiftly and neatly to the other foot, which instantly initiates the upward route that will carry us via an inside curve leading us (with a telling hesitation just long enough to register the intelligence in the face) onward again to the papers, back to the starting point: the ideas.

Examining the figure itself, we see pride and commitment depicted in the facial expression, perhaps touched with a certain awe at the final feat he holds in his hand; the forehead is unfurrowed, the chin strong and the eyes piercing. The raised hand, proclaiming victory, holds the documents firmly but naturally, as by *right*, needing the sanction of no higher authority. Fixing our attention on the force pulsing through the raised arm for one instant more, as if defying the heavens above, the poetically inclined of us might speculate (and Frudakis has confirmed) that the sculptor positioned the victorious arm of his figure consciously in remembrance of (and contrast to) the powers of the Sky god Zeus, mightiest of the ancient Greek gods, whose thunderbolt was believed to direct the course of all worldly events from the lightning streak of supremacy issued at his command. Here the godly power is transformed into that of an earthly man, who is made mighty by intellection and animated by the ideological energy of a mental bolt of thunder charging into a document of enlightenment, proclaiming values that would direct the course of history toward an understanding of *inalienable* rights.

Externally, the details of clothing worn by *The Signer* are meticulous and accurate for their era without being ornamental; they define rather than conceal the nude body, which stretches the seams of the fabric upward beneath its jubilant motion. The virility and health of the body, lean and agile and full of prime-of-life energy, thus becomes accentuated by the clothes rather than hidden by them. This is *man* in all his brilliance, at the height of his capacities, physically, mentally, morally and spiritually. Yet incredibly, as the figure strains, bursting with mastery against his garments, we become aware that, in spite of its inherent strengths, the physical body is vulnerable. As this knowledge breaks silently and soberly into our consciousness, we are moved to marvel in a different way at the courage displayed by every fragile breath of this hero's being—not only his name but his very corporeal survival goes on the line with his signing. Furthermore, because the sculptor has clearly gone so far out of his way aesthetically to remind us of the nude form, we are impelled to accept that we are meant to view this single historical figure as a universal one, representative of all individuals at their best. Nevertheless, the fact remains that (obviously) this *is* an historical figure commemorating an historical moment in time; therefore, if we wish to learn the full context of its creation, we must now turn for more information to

Subject:

The 12½-foot figure (its size is also a clue to its intended universality and heroism) may be found outside Independence Hall in Philadelphia. Standing before it, we do not need to see its name engraved on the stone base or read the plaque on a nearby wall to be persuaded that we are witnessing that unparalleled moment in time when America was born. If we look closely, we may notice that the figure holds *two* documents in his hand and if we know our history, we will understand that the sculptor chose George Clymer of Philadelphia to represent all of the signers because Clymer was the only one to sign both the Declaration of Independence and the Constitution of the United States. [The monument was commissioned by the Independence Hall Association and donated to the City of Philadelphia in 1982 to celebrate its tri-centennial birthday, so the sculptor subtly and sensitively honored one of the City's own great sons while simultaneously honoring all of the brave men who signed their names to their values.] At the same time, viewing the surging spirit of this one figure frozen in time, we cannot help but fathom deep in our souls that this monument honors more than that moment and those men. It is a salute to all men and women who ever have or ever will "sign" their values by taking the necessary actions to achieve them in real life. It is a tribute to the past and a promise to the future that the indomitable spirit of man combined with ideas founded in reason *will* prevail.

We are now prepared by our own personal observations and interactions to read the words on the plaque, which confirm what we have already absorbed through our eyes and assimilated into our minds:

> Certain rare moments change the course of history. Yet within a mere eleven years, two such moments, the signing of the Declaration of Independence and the signing of the Constitution of the United States occurred in Independence Hall, just a few steps from where you are standing. The sculpture you see before you commemorates the courage of those who altered their lives, and ours, by affixing their names to these documents.
>
> Inspired by George Clymer, Philadelphia merchant, statesman, and signer of both the Declaration of Independence and the Constitution of the United States, "The Signer" commemorates the spirit and deeds of all who devoted their lives to the cause of American Freedom.

What an experience it is to interact with great art! We may love it or hate it—that is a subjective reaction based on each of our own value systems, and the level of passion we feel "aye" or "nay" expresses the fierceness with which we hold our values dear to us. But art at its best will always command our attention by *addressing* the most fundamental aspects of reality and the human condition. It also reveals the value system of the artist who created it in the same instant that we confess our own philosophical base by our responses to it. Great art evokes our emotions, for better or for worse, by stimulating our minds. It lets us see and touch and hear our own deepest values in physical form, as perceived through our senses.

For this reason above all others, serious art is not and never has been a luxury; it is a psychological and spiritual (even an epistemological) necessity. If the art is good, it offers us a time-stopped vision of reality *heightened* by the conscious combination and manipulation of aesthetic and value choices made by the artist in order to communicate a chosen theme. The (thoughtful) artist is in effect saying to us, "Stop. Look. Listen. This is *important*." The greater the ideas informing the art, the greater the art. If the artist has no content at all at the core of his work, it is easy to judge it banal; pretty pictures, even if beautifully rendered, are decorative art. To stay with the visual arts—although every art form accomplishes the same thing by inventively implementing its particular, aesthetic vocabulary—we can see that from an intellectually complex work like *The Signer* to one depicting a nature scene like, for example, a simple (it never is!) seascape or flower arrangement, art encourages us to look at, listen to, and think more astutely about *life*. *David*, *The Thinker* and *The Signer* present images of the human circumstance. A seascape suggests we look with a keener eye at nature—did we ever really notice *that* color of green in the water before?—and a floral still-life may guide our vision the next time we walk through our own garden, or even give us pause to ponder the transience of every living thing, including ourselves...all to our immense pleasure and benefit. Interacting with art helps us interact with life by sharpening our senses and our powers of observation, by stimulating thought and by inspiring us to *new* thought.

Because of the unparalleled necessity of art, an argument may well be made that the teaching of the subject should be part of the mandatory curricula in schools: instead of the three "R's," four: **R**eading, W**R**iting, A**R**ithmetic *and* A**R**t. [See speech: *The Fourth "R" in Education*, page 127.] For by learning the craft—the discipline of form—of any art, be it drawing, playing an instrument or composing a poem, we can learn how to employ reason and express ideas through another "language" that is, although more indirect, as powerful as words. Through art we can learn how to "bring to life," to make manifest in a physically accessible and especially beautiful concrete form even the deepest conceptual abstractions. Art—whether creating or appreciating it— teaches us to esteem the beauties, the wonders, and the mysteries of reality *and ourselves* on a much higher level so we may enrich our daily life experiences with more meaning and greater pleasure. By learning how to "see," to comprehend, and to judge a work of art in all its parts—in the visual arts: form, subject matter and content—we may enrich our understanding of ourselves and the world in which we live in a unique manner, one that not only fires our own imagination to new creativity but also inspires us to *know* that in a great work of art, as in life itself, the whole is so much greater than the sum of its parts.

He who has imagination without learning has wings but not feet.

Chinese Fortune Cookie

The Fourth "R" in Education:
Reading, WRiting, ARithmetic and ARt

This speech was first delivered at the Center for Constructive Alternatives conference "Art and Moral Imagination," Hillsdale College, Hillsdale, Michigan, November 3, 1997. It was published in Vital Speeches of the Day, *February 15, 1998 and (edited) in* Imprimis, *June 1998. It was later delivered by Ms. York at an Arts in Education conference in Oklahoma City sponsored by the Foundation for Academic Excellence, October of 1999 and again at CommonGround Parent Association of Princeton Area of Independent Schools, in November of the same year.*

I want to tell you a story. Early one morning, a man was walking along a bluff overlooking the ocean when he noticed a barefoot woman walking along the beach clearly engrossed in a strange activity: she was picking up star fish that had been washed ashore by the tide, and one by one, throwing them back into the sea. Intrigued, he scrambled down the bank of the cliff and approached her. "What are you doing?" he asked.

"I'm saving star fish," she answered, gently tossing another into the water.

The man let his eyes drift over the endless shoreline in wonder. "But," he stammered, "there are *thousands* of star fish stranded on this beach. You can't save them all!"

"I know," the woman smiled. She picked up another star fish and returned it to the ocean. "But I'm saving *this* one." She continued undaunted. "And this one. And this one."

Dear friends, colleagues, teachers and students, those star fish languishing on the barren sand are the youth of America. And they have been swept up onto the beachhead of ignorance and sloth by the tide of our failed progressive educational system. It falls to us now, those of us who do understand the deep purposes of education, to save the future of our country. We can do this by returning our children, one by one, back to the sea of *structured* creativity, where each individual child—by nature of being a child—can be taught to swim smartly, successfully, and joyfully toward the promise of adulthood. To accomplish this task, I propose that we incorporate art education into the mandatory school curricula. I propose art instruction because *only* art educates the whole person as an integrated individual: it educates the senses, it educates the mind, and it educates the emotions. It educates the soul.

Before we set to exploring this proposal, however, I wish to say "Thank you" to Hillsdale College for inviting me to share my thoughts on "Art and the Moral Imagination" with you during this five day conference. And I thank *you* for coming this evening to share both the art and the ideas expressed in *The Legacy Lives* art exhibit. It was on this very stage where, five years ago, I announced the formation of the American Renaissance for the Twenty-first Century arts foundation. I marvel at the good distance we have come since that day in 1992, and I am grateful to all those who have helped in our many achievements, including this exhibit. Our mission of promoting a rebirth of beauty and life-affirming values in all of the fine arts is, of course, not only for the purpose of improving the arts but also for the purpose of elevating our culture as a whole. It is an ambitious mission and the challenges are great.

These challenges take many forms. Not just in the arena of the fine arts, but even more fundamentally, in the arena of ideas—especially in our educational system. Let us remember that the three old fashioned "Rs" of education—readin', ritin' and 'rithmetic—were not instituted in schools to help the populace read the daily papers, write letters home to Mom, and pay bills owed the general store. These primary skills were and *should* be taught for the larger purpose of instructing young people to think and to function in the real world for the rest of their lives in a rational, efficacious, self-sufficient and self-satisfying manner. School should prepare young people for *life*.

Reading (literature and history in particular) teaches the

ability to comprehend the world and man's place in it; writing is the means of any serious communication and teaches the ability to crystallize thoughts and communicate them objectively; arithmetic (meaning the whole category of math) teaches the ability to measure attributes of entities in reality, thereby bringing all of the universe into perceptual grasp. These are the basics. In better schools, science is included, and in many schools, physical education usually rounds out the mandatory program, which is good except where—too often!—soccer dominates syntax. Too often, too, a serious education in the three basics is not really mandatory anymore, meaning that the courses are regularly adulterated for political correctness, diluted of solid grounding in rudimentary skills, and short-shrifted as subjects for prolonged study, all of which in turn defeat the purpose of required subjects.

In fact, in light of today's permissive educational environment, we might need to remind ourselves of why certain studies should be mandatory in the first place. It used to be a truism—and it is still true—that students do not yet know enough to know what they don't know; therefore, adults specializing in the teaching of knowledge, along with parents, should set the principal standards of their education. Once again, this presumes that a certain level of knowledge and ability in basic subjects is necessary to pursue an informed life on an independent basis after graduation from school and separation from family homes.

It is with these thoughts in mind that I propose the addition of art education to the three basics. I should clarify, here, that I mean art education founded in the established Western art forms. The reason for focusing on art forms evolving from our Western heritage is that the forms themselves (the physical presentations) are the most malleable, with the richest aesthetic vocabulary for expressing the most complex ideas. This kind of art—begun with the Greeks and carried on through the Renaissance to the nineteenth century, sadly skipping most of the twentieth but resurfacing with vigor as we approach the millennium—can be defined as an intelligible representation of the world and humankind that manifests an artist's conceptual visions in perceptual, aesthetic form.

The primary arts, as we all know, are painting, sculpture, poetry, literature, drama, music and architecture, the last of which is unique because it combines its art form with functional use. A modicum of working knowledge in all of the arts will facilitate an appreciation of them, but protracted study in the visual arts (drawing, painting and sculpture), creative writing (poetry, drama and short story) and music (instrument and music appreciation) are critical for advanced perceptual and conceptual development, so these may best constitute the base triad for art education.

Why should the teaching of this art become the fourth "R"? Because to teach art is to teach life. Each lifetime, in its own way, has a "theme," an ever unfolding personal destiny, self-scripted by each individual depending on how they decide to approach and fill the hours of their days. Every (good) work of art does the same: first, it is an idea in the mind of the artist—a mental abstraction, a vision seen through the mind's "eye," an imaginative summation of the images and ideas wished to be expressed. Then it goes through the aesthetic process of transformation from that mental vision into a physical object (or in the case of the literary arts and music, a finite time experience) that can be perceived through the senses and the intellect of others, that can be *understood*. Finally, it takes on a life of its own to be enjoyed and considered as an individual entity—an end in itself—just like every human being. Because humans have free will, they choose their values by a process of selection; this is why character development and the development of art are so similar—they are both self created. Thus learning a demanding art form promotes both a curiosity and confidence that can be transferred to real life situations.

How does it do this? Let's take the benefits of art education one at a time: Sensory education, using the visual arts (painting) as our example; mental education, using creative writing as our example; and emotional education, using music as our example. These examples should not be construed as being exclusive of one another. Happily, each art form augments the lessons learned in all the others to educate the whole person. Each has its own aesthetic vocabulary, each appealing primarily to a different sense organ: painting and sculpture to sight (with sculpture adding the tangible sense of touch), music to hearing, and the most complex arts such as fiction appealing to all of the combined senses through imagination. Equally important, every art form is rooted in a discipline of craft, and learning the techniques of any craft teaches purpose, structure, observation, selectivity of essentials, and judgment of execution with verifiable outcome. In other words, the proficiency of means employed as well as the end result can be assessed via objective criteria. Furthermore, disciplined but ductile art forms can be endlessly manipulated and stylized to provide aesthetic emphasis as well as to dramatize ideational content.

To take our first example: we can readily grasp how creating what seems to be the simplest of paintings requires knowledge of drawing, color, shape, composition and perspective—knowledge derived not only from technical training but also from close observation of reality. Once a student has learned to render the three dimensional world of nature in this two dimensional form, enjoyment and appreciation of the real world automatically become enriched with ever keener observations. In order to paint a single tree, we really have to *look* at it. How a young person's sense of *seeing* will be improved! What nuances of the color green alone will he notice in the future because of these acute observations, not just in nature but in man-made objects as common as clothing, cars and tableware? What varieties of textures, edges and shapes gleaned from scrutinizing fragile, scalloped leaf formations will enhance his everyday experience of the patterns made by interlacing shadows, the woven surfaces of fabrics, or the eyelashes of a newborn infant? Even to imitate nature we must observe her; each student of painting—one by one, remember?—will gain life awareness by these observations.

Moving up one level, to *interpret* nature through painting, consciously creating (let's say) a mood will benefit students even more because it requires developing a process of selection in order to fulfill a larger intention, that of endowing the work with significance. Subject matter is then employed indirectly to express... something more. Now, questions arise as to *which* observations are most relevant to that deeper intention. Those graceful veins in the leaves, are they important enough to delineate or should she just suggest them? What of the bark sheathing the trunk? Since she wants a serene feeling, should she apply the paint thinly with light brushstrokes to de-emphasize the rough surface? In order to create an atmosphere that stresses the mysteries of nature, should she push the blue of the sky toward violet? Because this next level of art teaches how to formulate a *hierarchy* in the selection of essentials, entailing judgment at every turn, it prompts questions and demands problem solving, sensitizing powers of discrimination and increasing attention span for contemplation of the relative importance of all things in life, large and small.

Thus we see that inherent within the process of exercising their sense perceptions, students must by necessity also exercise their minds. And beyond this first horizon of sense-mind interplay lies the limitless vista of the imagination. Meaningful art is not just mimesis of life as it is or even an expressive rearrangement; it is an inquiry into the human condition, of man's desires and dreams, fears and fantasies. Important art is important because it is multi-layered, stimulating our senses, touching our hearts and awakening our minds to verities and possibilities. Aesthetics, then, become the means to art's supreme end: content. Content is inseparable from the underlying theme(s) of a work; it is that, but it is so much, much more: Ultimately, it is the human spirit incarnate—the shimmering breath of light streaming from a thoughtful artist's mind and hands and soul that, through meticulous crafting, becomes a theme illuminating itself. It resides within and emanates from the art as a pure result of the artist's most purposeful and personal imbuing of it with intelligent meaning, with ideas. It is *great* art's anima: both source and sum, it is the substantive realization of an artist's deepest values, true or false, good or bad, beautiful or ugly. And here is where the moral imagination enters fully into the creative process, for even a novice approach to this highest level of art educates the mind philosophically.

Let's use creative writing as an example. Because literature is a conceptual transmission from the mind of a writer to the mind of a reader it becomes, whether via a wide avenue or a narrow labyrinth, an enchanting passage to the imagination—a journey of ideas not to what is but to what could and might be. Good fiction compels us to weave a theme through the events of a story and the actions of the characters. Assuming craft, the more universal and fundamental the theme, the greater the fiction. Assuming theme—unfortunately, most fiction today, as most art in general, lacks theme—but assuming theme, we imagine interlocking scenes in our imagination first, and then heightened visions of all that is possible in the world are activated in our minds as we write. Gradually, as we learn to distill our thoughts and communicate through the techniques of narrative, description, dialogue, metaphor and dramatization, our imaginations are freed to create whatever we can dream up! New questions arise: Is this idea true? How is truth determined? Is it relevant to all human beings or just a few? Or only me? Are my characters understandable? Are they behaving morally or immorally, and why? Are their actions motivated by *their* value system?

Because the written arts are conceptual in form, students have an opportunity (even in creating a nursery rhyme, a dramatic skit or a fairtale) to explore the moral imagination directly. An artist's value system is consciously or unconsciously inherent in every work of art. This is so precisely because, as we have seen, the process of creating art requires constant choices of everything from subject matter to size. But creative writing requires the student to pay special attention to the internal lives of fictional, "made-up" individuals. How do we make up fictional human beings so as to render them believable? By infusing their thoughts, utterances and actions with *values*. As readers we understand that we come to "know" fictional people largely the same way we learn to know real-life people: we discern their underlying "character" by observing and listening to them. A rational person selects his or her values through the use of reason and logic, making sure that the values are consonant with nature and human nature. If they are, they will be life-serving values. If they are life-serving values, they will be moral. If a person (or a character) *acts* only on rational values, their actions will be moral. If their actions are moral, *they* will be moral. If we wish to present an immoral character, we will create a fictional person who acts consciously against sound values. And just think of all the inbetweens, the conflicted characters! By learning writing skills, students can play out real life conflicts in an imaginative setting with imagined people. Talk about a chance to explore ideas, issues, behavior and psychology in a safe environment!

As the visual arts train the senses by honing our physical perceptions of the world, so the art of writing trains the mind by demanding concept formation and a philosophical view of the world. If students are engaged in both art forms, what they learn in one will reinforce what they learn in the other, beginning an interactive process with incalculable power to foster discreet subtleties of awareness and sensitivity (literally!) in every walk of life. In addition, incidental but important side benefits of all art study are learning to be alone, enjoying the *kairos* of life by becoming involved in the act of creation to the point of forgetting time as *chronos*; learning to experiment uninhibitedly with various options; learning to follow curiosity not only for the purpose of inventing but also for the adventure of discovering; learning to approach effort as pleasure, work as pleasure, and challenge as pleasure.

Lastly, but perhaps first in today's world of rampant subjectivism and temperamental indulgence, the arts educate the emotions. Not everyone is passionate—passion is the fervent intensity of emotion one experiences only when one commits the highest level of devotion to values—but everyone has feelings, if only instinctual fear or desire. And all feelings, whether complex or primitive, mentally inspired or physically excited, can be conveyed productively and safely through the *structure* of an art form. In this way, pubescent youngsters in particular can learn to deal constructively with feelings often so strong they don't know what to do with them; they can actually "work them out" through the creation of their art. This doesn't mean "express yourself" wallowing nor does it mean psychotherapy. It means healthy emotional flowering. It means psychological growth.

All art training nurtures this, but music is indispensable for guiding psychological development because it speaks directly to the sentient consciousness. One might say that music *is* emotions, because feelings are its primary themes. The instrument chosen to channel music's emotional flow, whether it be piano, clarinet, violin or voice, is not important. Learning to play the instrument *is*. The discipline of serious music is exact and exacting, teaching the precision of math in a poetic realm, teaching both the exhilarating balance and the exalted integration of "reasoned harmony" (music's form) and emotions (music's content). It is not often in our culture that children are taught to unite reason and emotions. Tonal, melodic classical music does this for all of us. So the competence to *hear* it, to appreciate it to a degree made possible by knowing how to play any instrument, can be a rare source of indescribable pleasure and safe emotional release for the child now and the adult later.

Like life, musical passages contain highs and lows, fast

and slows, and musical vocabulary includes dissonance and resolution, tumult and sublimity, all emboldening a student in the process of making music to *feel* to his heart's content within the security of a confined experience. There is no way to fall out of control because the rhythm keeps the music going—the notes must be played on time and accurately—affording an expansive opportunity to learn to channel emotions into a finite structure with a finite time limit. By learning to orchestrate emotional content through so rigorous a structure, the student *must* learn to merge reason and emotions; otherwise, the resulting music will be cold and sterile, math without the poetry. Classical music is too mentally commanding to permit the flailing and screaming incited by rock n' roll, thus it forces young people to control their emotional output, offering them the experience of cathexis rather than catharsis. Also, because music deals with broad abstractions—triumph, defeat, love, loss—it allows a young person to personalize universals of the human condition, to feel on a grand scale both the hope and the hurt that necessarily accompany an individual life fully lived. For teenagers, in particular, it unlocks gateways to *mature* excursions into the ecstacy and the vulnerability of love, the headiness and the hazards of risk. Often, once young people begin to understand the value of classical music, they turn to it in moments of emotional need to help them experience deep stirrings that may not make it to the surface of consciousness by themselves. Repressed boys, especially, can benefit immensely from music study.

So we begin to see the vital importance of art education, the invigorating and reinforcing spiral of experience inherent in learning the various art forms. Back and forth, from real life to art, from art form to art form and back to real life, the senses, the intellect and the emotions flow together, charging each other along the way with images, sounds and ideas. Students of art become students of life. And *this* should be our goal. Once they experience the arduous bliss of making art, some will pursue it as a profession, of course. But the purpose of art study is not to make artists out of our young people; it is to help them become complete human beings.

Youth is forward motion. And the arts can forever inspire this forward motion because they are open ended and can continue indefinitely to absorb our natural creative energies. No art form can ever be entirely mastered because the techniques can always be further expanded and exploited, so skills and appreciation learned while we are still chronologically young can serve us our whole lives long. As we grow and develop as human beings, we can continue for a lifetime stretching our capabilities through artistic expression, if only as a casual hobby or through spectator appreciation on a high level. Our bodies will age and our physical prowess (in sports, for example) will diminish, but our minds and our imaginations need never grow old. Practical knowledge of the arts can keep us forever active mentally, psychologically and emotionally, learning, growing, advancing...the very hallmarks of youth.

Let us insist that our children be offered these priceless opportunities provided by art education. Whether they want it or not. Mandatory, remember? My own father used to tell me it was his responsibility as a parent to "introduce" me— that meant I *had* to do it—to certain things in life that would help me become a worthy human being. I began ballet at three, piano at five, acting at seven, and voice (on my own) in college—Making up stories and plays I always did on my own. I was required to bring home one book a week from the library throughout grade school—Did you know that the girl detective *Nancy Drew* is still on the shelves? My brother and I were required to taste everything set out on the dinner table. If we weren't fond of some particular food, we could ask our mother for a "courtesy helping," which meant one level tablespoon. If we made a face or said something negative, we got another tablespoon—I remember eating a whole bowl of parsnips that way one night—until we learned to acquire a taste for the flavor or at least moderate our behavior. Today, there is not a single food I do not savor.

It is my observation, these days, that many parents and teachers are afraid of children. You don't need to beat children into doing what's best for them; you can negotiate something you want for them with something they want for themselves. You *do*, however, need to inculcate the habit of cooperation in them while you're still bigger than they are! In my early childhood I disliked piano, but if I wanted dance lessons (which I loved) I had to stick with piano as well. When, in my mid-teens, I finally terminated music lessons, I was glad (as I am now) that I could entertain myself by playing the instrument respectably and appreciate others' playing of it as well.

Another observation, obvious to anyone, is that parents (and even grandparents) today emulate their children instead of setting examples for them. By dressing like kids in jeans, sneakers and message tee-shirts, wearing baseball caps during dinner, reducing their own vocabularies to mindless street jargon—"hey," "cool," "no problem," "Hi guys,"—by listening incessantly to blaring primitive music, what do parents think they are offering their children regarding the refinements of adulthood?—a state of achieved maturity that they, by the way, are pathetically missing themselves. No wonder America has become a nation of aging adolescents!

I suggest to you that the nation's schools could not have failed, as they have, unless mothers and fathers failed first by abdicating their parental responsibility as guardians of their children's inner development. Now, it is past time for concerned parents to assume their obligation *as* parents and set the standards for the education of their own children. Art education is *crucial*. It can be taught privately, of course, but instituting it into school systems, public or otherwise, is not as formidable as you might think. There are hundreds of prototype parent groups all over the country doing just this by forming nonprofit organizations that fundraise and contribute money to schools targeted *only* for the purpose of incorporating the arts into the curricula. If anyone wants specific information on this, please contact me personally.

Finally, may I say that although Americans largely do not understand this, art is not a luxury, it is a necessity...a spiritual one. At its apotheosis aesthetically, philosophically and psychologically, art provides a spiritual summation by integrating mind and matter—abstract values perceived by the senses. When form and content are exquisitely unified in art to express the most universal truths via the most beautiful physical presentation in the most technically proficient manner, art offers an experience of complete concinnity, a harmoniously integrated experience of mind, body and soul—both to its maker and to its worthy beholder. Thus it is the very souls of our emotionally abandoned, value starved youth that we can rescue through art education. For it is art that best teaches the moral imagination everywhere apparent in the different art forms, through which the soul of the artist, young or old, professional or amateur or student, is revealed. But, just like the star fish we can rescue them only one at a time, for every child like, every adult is a precious, fragile, unrepeatable, *individual* being. Shan't we nourish each soul with the beauty, the wonder and the delight of the mind as carefully as we nourish each body with bread, milk and honey? The thirteenth-century Persian poet Muslih-uddin Sadi counseled us thus:

> If of thy mortal goods thou art bereft
> And from thy slender store
> Two loaves alone to thee are left
> Sell one, and with the dole
> Buy hyacinths to feed thy soul

Yes! It is the beauty of art and the arts of beauty that feed the human spirit by making the invisible visible and the visible *more* visible, affirming the value of visions, visions that bring values to life. Art and the moral imagination? Art *is* the moral imagination.

All of our yesterdays are summarized in our now, and all the tomorrows are ours to shape.

Hal Borland

Art as Spiritual Experience

First Published in ART Ideas, *Volumn 5,
Number 3, Autumn 1998.*

When Mr. A gazes at a painting of a purple-hued mountain range in winter, sculpted against a quivering blue sky that seems brushed in long sweeps of red, yellow and orange by the rays of a setting sun, he feels swept joyously into that scene to the degree that he surrenders all sense of himself as a separate being and becomes an integral part of it, feeling that the world at this moment is perfect and that he is the last piece of the puzzle *making* it perfect, making it complete and whole—that he is part of something so right, so beautiful, so good and true that it seems equally a part of him.

When Miss B looks at the same painting, she feels joyous, too, but rather than "entering" the scene to become part of it, she feels empowered to conquer it, to climb those mountains, to reach their peak, to reach *her* peak—her body tenses for action, her breath comes in staccato snatches—there is nothing she can't do at this moment.

Miss C, standing right next to Miss B but blithely unaware of her, regards the painting and feels suspended in time, suspended in a quiet hush heightened by an exquisite sense of physical and mental well being, suspended in a serene state of perfect harmony so beautiful and peaceful that she cannot imagine any evil or suffering anywhere in the universe.

Mr. D passes by the mountainscape without notice, drawn irresistibly to a floral still life, suddenly—achingly—overwhelmed by the preciousness of *all* life as expressed in the image of one fragile flower, a preciousness that fills and fills him until he thinks he will physically burst from the benevolence he feels toward every living thing in the universe.

What shall we call these supremely positive emotional/physical responses to art? Words seem so superfluous and inadequate to describe these feelings of ecstacy that permeate and thrill both mind and body. To what else shall we compare them? Why do they feel so personal? These feelings are far and away above day-to-day emotional reactions. Why?

And what will *you* feel when you view the same scene as described above? Or if like Mr. D you pass it by, which painting or work of sculpture will make you catch *your* breath and set off a sequence of interactions that take you straight to the summit of your being?

Throughout history, art has served many and various functions, from religions' handmaiden to a recording of people, places and events, but its pre-eminent non-utilitarian function has been and always will be that of stimulating a spiritual experience in both its creator and its beholder.[1] Most people tend to think of spirituality in terms of religious or mystical experiences, where one's own "spirit" is deemed to connect literally with an (immaterial) omnipotent Force or supernatural Spirit. But exalted feelings of sanctity and the sublime can be evoked on a secular level too, inspired by (among other significant things) art that makes manifest our most personal core value system.

As we all know, each of the fine arts appeals to a particular sense organ—painting to sight, sculpture to sight and touch, music to hearing, and so on. The visual arts, however, may be the most accessible of all art forms because (unlike music or drama, for example, which are "played out" over a period of time) they deliver the sum of their aesthetics and their content all at once, which has the power to elicit an immediate reaction on the part of the viewer. The visual arts are also quite easy to decipher aesthetically and intellectually. So if you wish to explore the subject of spiritual experience through art, a museum is a good place to start.

Before getting to some practical guidelines for a sojourn to the spiritual via art, some overview of the subject may be in order.

I considered searching for or devising a term other than "spirituality" to designate secular experiences of exaltation precisely because of the above-mentioned associations with religion or otherworldliness. Especially in our present culture where a spiritual search is *on*—fundamentalism-cultism and Eastern religions *cum* New Age compete directly with traditional Western religions for adherents, so the word is considerably overloaded as never before with connotations of immaterial transcendence. Nevertheless, I have chosen to retain the terminology for two reasons: (1) it is accurate and must not be relinquished to only mystical-whatever-the-persuasion usage, and (2) in virtually every religion or mystical system the word implies some sort of connection to the *highest*, whatever that might be perceived to be; it is in this sense that I use the word here, not to compete with mysticism but to limn the highest experiences of earthly connection to oneself and one's most cherished values. [In this particular essay, I have modified spirituality with the adjective "secular" only to differentiate it from its religious overtones; in normal usage (in my view), it does not need modification as context alone should signal its meaning.]

The Oxford English Dictionary recognizes secular spirituality in several subtle ways, but the following among its various definitions are the most explicit: "Of or pertaining to, emanating from, the intellect or higher faculties of the mind; intellectual." and "Characterized by or exhibiting a high degree of refinement of thought or feeling." It is in the "spirit" of these definitions that we may include our loftiest art experiences. [In another dissimilar but hauntingly pertinent definition the O.E.D. suggests: "Of or pertaining to breathing; respiratory..." which is an obsolete meaning but fascinating because changes in breathing patterns often accompany spiritual experiences of all kinds.]

My own definition of secular spirituality—rooted thoroughly in Aristotelian naturalism—for our present purpose is as follows: a heightened state of being: a psycho-sensory experience of unity with one's own fundamental values in response to a physical entity embodying them, such as nature, art, or another person, which results from a process of mind-body integration.

In other words, the experience is begun by our over-whelmingly positive response to a real here-on-this-earth "other" material entity and completed by each of us in our own particular way as we mentally absorb the ideational content of the entity and integrate it intuitively[2] into our own particular value system. The experience is keenly person-alized not only because our own primary values are being stimulated but also in light of our specific background knowledge, associations, preferences, fears and dreams, which of course, are different for each of us. It is, after all, our individualized value systems, our mental methodology for processing information, our personal style (*very* important[3]) and our background knowledge and experiences that make each of us unique and unrepeatable human beings. Thus, we each bring all that we have become to every experience in life. But the most compelling, all-encompassing "peak" experiences must be called spiritual because they bring our inmost mind, the essential animating principles which we hold as the vital center of life, stirringly to the surface of our consciousness via an irresistible flow of emotions that radiates to one degree or another throughout our entire sentient being.

Nature offers us a banquet of *everything* in the physical world, so at any time of any day we can respond selectively with sublime appreciation to those particular aspects of nature's wonders which exemplify *our view* of the universe. Regarding art, an artist (whether painter, sculptor, writer, or composer) controls the "nature" of his man-made "universe"—his work of art—and consciously or uncon-sciously[4] imbues it with his values. If those values are also our own and if the work is aesthetically compelling to us, we can interact with its thematic content to see or hear our own (conceptual) values personified in concrete form. The combination must be just right: content, form and style, the last being the most intrinsic of all. In the case of romantic love and its physical (sexual) concomitant, we respond to another person of like soul both philosophically and stylistically—The same process occurs in friendship but without the romantic element because although a friend can be a soulmate, there is no physical attraction which promotes a mind-body connection.

Depending on context, all of these responses have the potential to instantaneously generate in us exquisite feelings of whole-self celebration. These peak psychological-physiological experiences are, in fact, our greatest reward for the hard work we have done in rationally selecting (rather than accumulating) our values. Here and only here may we celebrate our earthly selves in totality, with no reservations. We are experiencing moments of perfect union, of complete integration of mind and matter brought about by our responses to physical stimuli and our one-on-one interaction with both its form and its content.

Neuroscientists are making some fascinating discoveries concerning just how such processes work biologically. This is outside the scope of our present delimited subject, but I mention it to alert those who may have interest in probing that area. It obviously isn't necessary to understand all of the mechanics in order to experience these consummate feelings of "oneness" with the physical world, or with the worldview expressed in art, or with another person...and always, at these moments, with ourselves. There is no dualistic "mind-body problem" here because we are mind and body unified, and we know that we are far more than atoms in motion. We feel so replete with heightened awareness, both emotionally and physically, so generous, as if everything is so right, pure, good and true. The sense of immediate self identification in this process is "key" because it is that connection that opens us emotionally to a sense of feeling "I am an indivisible part of this perfect whole,"[5] or "I *am* this," or "This is *me*." It's like witnessing oneself—rejoicing in oneself—outside of one's self, and through the process of loving "another," we love ourselves.[6]

At times like these one has no sense of escaping the real world but of embracing it in all its splendor; the focus of attention is so complete that we are aware only of the absolute joy in being fully alive. At times like these we are unaware of our age, race, physical appearance, or any other detail of our existence—We feel beautiful and we *are* beautiful.

Spiritual experiences of this nature, activated by the physical world, a work of art or another person are secular because they rely utterly on external stimulation of each individual's unique set of values to unlock mental doors to the experience; hence, these types of experiences can be enjoyed by all people regardless of religious affiliation.

Religious experiences are usually evoked through predetermined images and/or rituals codified in holy texts or through instruction by an elite body such as shamans, priests, rabbis and gurus. In addition, where secular spirituality relies solely on physical entities to trigger the psycho-sensory response, many religious or mystical experiences appear to come unbidden and often have a revelatory quality to them, a sense of sudden insight that comes with such certainty— the soul *is* immortal and there *is* life after death, for example— that it feels received from an outside Source, requiring no participation on the part of the receiver. In contrast, secular experiences are highly participatory because we must mentally process and integrate physically stimulated value recognition directly into the moral center of our one-and-only individual being without symbols, rituals or previous teaching. We might say (without being flip) that secular spiritual experiences are more customized than mystical experiences. Very religious people will, of course, see God's hand or God's calling in everything great and small, but religious inclinations and beliefs do not in any way preclude nor conflict with secular spiritual experiences.

Conversely, people who hold reason as absolute, eschewing faith as an avenue to truth, may come to the false conclusion that spiritual experiences are something they can never have. They may assume that one must be religious or mystical or, in one fashion or another, suspend reason in order to achieve a spiritual state of being; therefore, even if they are overwhelmed by such an experience accidentally—which can happen—they are uncomfortable with it and shut it down, since it would appear to contradict their allegiance to reason. This is further complicated by the fact that many of these same people, who meticulously permit themselves only behavior they believe to be consonant with reason, are often reluctant to "let go" into an emotional experience of *any* kind for fear of "losing control" of their rational mind.

Ergo: Religious people may permit themselves religiously inspired spiritual experiences yet shy away from secular spirituality for fear they are straying from God, thus depriving themselves of powerfully personal experiences of a different kind. And non-religious people may shy away from spiritual experiences altogether for fear (because of the emotional vulnerability) they are straying from reason, thus depriving themselves of a cornucopia of pleasures to be experienced by opening themselves to hidden treasures waiting within. All of us—whatever our religious or philosophical persuasion—need spiritual experiences because they provide each of us the necessary inner joys of human existence. As comestibles nourish our bodies and ideas nourish our minds, so do spiritual experiences—the unification of these two aspects of our being, the integration of mind and body— nourish our souls, the vital essence of our *being*.

That being said, some general guidelines may be helpful to the uninitiated in seeking spiritual experiences through art. To begin at the beginning: Your choice of museum—or at least the wing or rooms you wish to explore—may prove a critical factor in successfully achieving any personal experiences at all, let alone those of emotional intensity. Large crowds and advertising hype may adversely affect your temperament (they do mine!), especially because many museums have become far more—or far less!—than repositories of works of art that offer the possibility of long quiet moments filled with pleasure and contemplation. As the art-viewing atmosphere becomes less serious and more social, it's sometimes difficult to ignore the museum race to keep up with our entire culture's becoming one big entertain-ment theme-park shopping mall. The larger institutions, especially, often focus on blockbuster exhibits for social cachet; singles bars (complete with music) for an upscale stop on the dating game or networking circuit; private space with complete catering services for partying; candle-lit restaurants for dining; lecture series for adult education or college credit; and retail outlets offering everything from books and art reproductions to tee-shirts and toys. All of this can distract our attention from the actual art that must be experienced on a one-on-one basis.

But forewarned is forearmed. You may wish to select a smaller museum (or at least beeline it straight to the sections you think most compatible with your own proclivities) or even an appropriate art gallery for your experiment into the more intimate experiences of art. With careful selection, the invitation to deeper pursuits *is* there in most fine museums, waiting patiently for each and every one of us, waiting within individual works of painting and sculpture that approach the sublime and *do* invite us to partake and participate in their beauty and their meaning. But regardless of locale, these we must always discover all by ourselves. Once having entered the general environment that beckons you, there are no maps, no rules and no rituals to guide you. This is a personal quest with no pre-determined direction or outcome. *You* are the "way," and only you can lead yourself.

Some specifics: Don't expect to find these live experiences in any art book or on TV (film, of course, can be one of the most potent art forms; it's just that it seldom rises to that level). Paintings and sculpture must be experienced in person; only then can you respond fully not only to subject matter or thematic content but also to the tangible aesthetic presentation and the scale of the work. Go alone. Don't put on any headphones! Don't read any signs or placards. Don't prejudge, preconceive or censor your reactions. *Do* let yourself "go." These private moments are a time to really trust yourself. After all, what would be the worst that could happen? It's not as if you're getting married to the wrong person. This is a quest for pleasure, self discovery and self celebration.

When entering any room, simply scan the art without pushing yourself. Let the art "speak" to you. There are no rights or wrongs in this adventure; open your mind to accept anything. When something draws your attention, whether it be subject matter or simply an arrangement of colors or shapes, stand or sit quietly before the work of art and think or feel everything—free associating—that comes to mind...or not. Feeling nothing in particular is fine, too, especially if this is your first time "out"; your quiet attention to something that calls you is a perfectly fine response. On the other hand, if you feel like laughing, do it. If you feel like weeping, do it. There can be many different levels of intensity within the broad spectrum of spiritual experiences of any kind, all the way from breathlessness, a pounding heart and emotional rapture to a calm and gentle inner hum. The more fundamental and complete the value identification the more profound the experience.

Be prepared for negative experiences as well as positive ones, knowing that if you feel moved to joy *or* anger by a work of art, one or more of your values are being confirmed or assaulted. If you feel true outrage—the opposite of spiritual joy—it is because the work offends your most fundamental core value system, your overall "worldview." The stronger you hold your values, the more passionate your responses will be one way or the other as those values are stimulated. Be aware, too, that your own style and psychological habits will determine your response to things to a great degree. To give a couple of examples: Let's say two different people are regarding the same seascape, each of them drawn initially to the work because of its subtle palette of muted colors and the dramatic, expressionistic brushstrokes. Upon closer inspection, however, it is determined that the muted colors are actually a heavy mist, nearly obscuring a lighthouse in the far distance. One person may now thrill at the mysteries inherent in the work—what *else* could be hidden from sight that would interest or excite me?—while the other may feel unsettled and annoyed for lack of being able to see clearly through the mist—I can't see the lighthouse! Maybe a ship can't see it either; this scene is full of impending danger. Or take a sculpture of Icarus fallen: One person may weep at the tragedy of the fall and another feel uplifted by the audacity of the flight.

Note negative reactions only to the extent that you may wish to revisit those works of art on another day in order to (intellectually) unravel their effect on you. For now, pay attention only to art that ignites unusually positive connections, that pleasures you to the highest degree. If you feel you are soaring with energy, or standing in blissful awe, or inspired and empowered, you are experiencing a moment of spiritual connection and identification with your own most private self—you are looking at yourself through the art and loving all that you see, within and without. Spend a couple of hours in this manner. Then have lunch or a cup of tea by yourself in the museum's restaurant—Try not to go outside the building. Let your mind wander to the art or any other subject; it doesn't matter. After your break, revisit *only* the art that caused you the most pleasure earlier. Let it work on you again and notice if you are now experiencing anything different or of a different intensity than before. Next, look carefully at the work. Are there any particular passages of line or other aesthetic features that especially please you? If the painting or sculpture has more than one figure, are certain figures of more importance to you than others? Is the surface treatment impressionistic or tight? Which do you like best? Since you haven't read any artists' names or titles of the works, give each work that has moved you a title (if you can), summing up its theme and why it is has touched you. Don't take any notes, let all this just "happen."

Because we live in a high tech, instant coffee world, too few of us take the time to pause for thoughtful reflection, to visit and replenish our own interior world of the spirit, which is so enriching an experience. Yet we *must* take the time if we wish to live fully. And if we are smart as well as sensitive, we can use these experiences to identify certain (perhaps heretofore unknown) subconscious assumptions that have risen to the surface of our awareness to cause powerful responses. This is not a suggestion for self therapy, but if we want to parlay the spiritual into an intellectual understanding of ourselves, we can make time (some other time) to introspect and explore our philosophical and psychological bases to great benefit. If there is nothing new to learn, we have learned the best news of all: that our conscious and subconscious values are the same, meaning we have done our homework and have become a fully-integrated person ready to savor our efforts with the greatest bonus of all: consummate pleasure in mind and body unified.

When I was twenty-three (already very familiar with spirituality in music, dance and the written arts, and even having many favorite paintings and sculptures at the Metropolitan Museum in New York), I visited the Louvre for the first time and experienced my first full-blown spiritual experience with a visual art. Sculpture was already a passion with me, especially Greek and Roman works I had seen at home. But there in Paris I found myself transfixed, rooted to a spot at the bottom of the main staircase in the (old) Louvre, literally physically unable to mount the stairs because I was totally mesmerized by the marble figure of *Nike of Samothrace* standing in all her glory at their summit, her powerful wings urging her forward, her gown's drapery flowing gracefully but energetically over her magnificent nude body, defining its shape rather than hiding it, her torso torqued for action, pulsing from the inner strength that inspires her to her purpose, her face intelligent and confident—Oh! she doesn't have a face nor even a head, it's been broken off—But that doesn't matter does it? because I am feeling *as* the "Winged Victory" feels...powerful and powerfully feminine. I am bristling with efficacious vitality yet sensuously aware of every delicious sinew of my body. I am all confident as a person and as a woman. My skin tingles with anticipation. My body can and will do whatever my mind commands, and my mind can command anything I can create. I can be victorious in all my endeavors; I can and I *will* because I *am* Victory. I mounted the stairs in awe. She was calling me. *I* was calling me—

Like a first love, a first deep art experience is never forgotten. We may move onward and upward to bigger and better experiences as we develop ourselves, but in some regard we may always use that first experience as some sort of bottom-line standard from which to judge all the rest.

If you haven't yet pursued these ultimate pleasures, waiting patiently for you in the world of art, why not set up an occasion for exploration soon? Surround yourself with art, people and nature that promote celebrations of the beauties and joys of the world and humankind...of *you*. Soul celebrations of this kind will enrich your everyday life by adding a dimension of inner satisfaction and peace that is unmatched in any other aspect of your life. Make time for them. Enjoy them. You have earned them.

1 All acts of honest life-enhancing creation are spiritual on one level or another; that's why artists become artists, so they can create exactly what they respond to; for example, when I write fiction or poetry, I write it in order that I may read it first.

2 Although most definitions of *intuitive* allude to some method of "knowing" that is outside the realm of reason, my definition is based solidly upon the integrative powers of the mind: a mental process of integration that decodes information at such a fast rate of speed we are not consciously aware of it; hence, the experience is one of "Ah, ha!" or of "knowing" something as a sum without being aware of the parts.

3 Style and physical presentation are highly significant elements in inciting spiritual experiences. We may appreciate the philosophical content of either art or another person, but that doesn't mean we fall completely under their "spell." The bravura of brushstrokes may entice one while it repels another; the drama of fiction may thrill one while making another feel uncomfortable; the feminine challenge of a strong woman may excite one man while turning off another; what one woman decides is confidence in a man, another may decide is arrogance. Style is crucial to falling in love with anything or anyone.

4 I mention this because many people hold one conscious view of existence and man's place in it, while simultaneously holding another, different or conflicting subconscious view of which they are unaware. All art preferences (whether painting, sculpture, music or fiction), are soul revealing precisely because they bypass conscious convictions and, through their different aesthetic forms appealing to our various senses, are routed directly from sense perception to the deepest reservoirs of our truest value system.

5 We are reminded that one of the etymological roots of the word "holy" is "whole" as in "complete".

6 See Aristotle's *Nichomachean Ethics*, Book Nine, for thought-provoking ideas on friendship and self love.

I am only one, but still I am one: I cannot do everything, but still I can do something; I will not refuse to do the something I can do.

Helen Keller

Art as Energy
for the Twenty-First Century

First published in Confrontation *Literary Journal, the 30th Anniversary Issue "Energy Thru, Energy Now," No. 66/67, Fall 1998/Winter 1999*

We have heard enough lamentation over twentieth century iconoclasm turned into nihilism. The time has come to focus on the opportunities that sparkle their promise among the debris of deconstruction. These nuggets of spirit, never lost though overwhelmed by postmodern rampages, remain so powerful that they offer hope and vitality as we march on to a new millennium and a new renaissance.

These are not empty words. We can meet the challenge of a renaissance—it has been met before—but in order to rise as a nation, we must each rise to our own best self individually. And how shall we find the energy for this blissfully arduous task? By fostering a rebirth of beauty and life-affirming values within the philosophical bedrock of our culture and championing art that manifests those values.

Because art acts as a shortcut to ideas (whether they be good or bad), it possesses irresistible puissance as a cultural force (for good or ill) by aesthetically concretizing abstract ideas, letting us see our values, touch them, and hear them in physical form, making them real. *Great* art is a vision of values that inspires us, elevates our spirits, projects possibilities—as Aristotle said, "a kind of thing that might be."

What "might be" artistically depends on what "might be" philosophically. About the first Renaissance, J. Bronowski wrote in *The Western Intellectual Tradition* (Harper & Brothers, 1960; reprinted, Dorset Press, 1986): "This above all is what the Renaissance did—to inspire men with a picture, the essential man, to which they themselves aspire. The Renaissance made ideas a new prime mover which could shape men and their societies, and the men, then, went on to reshape the ideas."

By making ideas a new "prime mover" applicable to all men and women, we must strive to identify the "essential man" in universal terms that take into consideration that which we are, as individuals, according to our human nature. As America becomes increasingly multicultural (not in its political correctness meaning but in the actual, physical sense of that term), those who will lead in the twenty-first century are likely to be those who direct our attention to the commonalities we all share as human beings *qua* human rather than perpetuating today's tribal mentality of group-think which seeks to turn race, religion, and gender circumstances into power/privilege centers.

Given this compelling context, which ideas shall be the best prime movers to generate a better future for all of us because it is better for each of us?

We know that a vibrant interest in antiquity was the leitmotif of the European Renaissance—both in art and in ideas; Greek humanism was ingeniously woven into Christianity until a rich tapestry of culture emerged. Today, the changing demographics of immigration into the United States offer different possibilities. In the past, newcomers to America (regardless of nationality) were predominately in some measure rooted in a white Euro-Judeo-Christian heritage, sharing similar values and ethical codes. This demonstrably is no longer the case as Hindus, Moslems, Buddhists—people of many different faiths, skin shades and cultural habits—become Americans. This influx of "foreign" influence (which will only increase) can bring great enrichment to our own rather homogeneous country, but it will also necessitate a high level of tolerance by all concerned if we are to live together in peace. It also necessitates an ever more universal, secular philosophy that pertains to each and all but does not infringe on various religious and cultural practices.

There has been much written about Neo-Platonic influence during the Italian experiment, which fit in well with the basic tenets of Christianity. But what about the humanism so prevalent during that same period—a deep concern for the human condition here on earth now? Aside from new knowledge about Greek and Roman art (both projecting humanistic viewpoints) which greatly influenced the period, let us recall that Thomas Aquinas introduced the naturalist ideas of Aristotle into the electrifying intellectual/artistic environment that became *the* Renaissance (so far), an explosively inventive period so powered by creative energy that it is cherished by all as a true Golden Age. This is important to remember because in the past two decades we have witnessed a fresh scholarly interest in Aristotelian thought, a phenomenon which stands in stark contrast to the 60s-generation-Eastern-influenced mysticism that has by now become almost mainstream in American culture.

Why this revival of Aristotle's ideas now? We might suggest that contemporary philosophers have found so many contradictions in modern philosophy that they have returned to Aristotle for a reliable tie to reality, but a good deal of interest has undoubtedly been provoked by an artist/thinker by the name of Ayn Rand (born in Soviet Russia in 1905 and an American by choice), who brought Aristotle's basic tenets to the forefront of our century's attention through her novels. Two of those books, *The Fountainhead* and *Atlas Shrugged*, have become classics, still selling over 300,000 copies a year, and according to a survey conducted by The Library of Congress and Book-of-the-Month Club, *Atlas* was named the second most important book of influence after the Bible. Although she wrote much nonfiction delineating her philosophical views (she died in 1982), it was through the themes, characters and plots of her fiction that she introduced serious philosophical ideas to her popular readers and, eventually, mobilized contemporary thinkers to pursue her philosophy of Objectivism in scholarly terms. In essence, her work energized intellectual pursuits of philosophers back toward Aristotle and away from modern philosophy's preoccupation with Plato and Kant. In addition, she expanded Aristotle's theses by focusing on an objective natural reality that provides a moral base for capitalism and rational self-interest without appeal to higher Authority.

As for the inextricable connection of art to ideas, Rand says in her 1969 book, *The Romantic Manifesto*: "art is the fuel and spark plug of man's soul; its task is to set a soul on fire and never let it go out. The task of providing that fire with a motor and a direction belongs to philosophy." Her work, because it married art and ideas, has inspired people to action, both philosophers and artists. Her art has generated new energy. Even to disagree with a serious thinker causes creative sparks to fly. This understanding of the crucial importance of exploring fundamental ideas *per se*—not postmodern politics or power plays—must become operative again if we are to rise anew.

At the same time Rand was breathing new life into philosophy by looking back to the ideas of Aristotle to inform her novels, a handful of artists, spurned by a post-World-War-II society increasingly infatuated with modernism and abstraction, kept alive the techniques of established Western heritage art forms: representationalism in painting and sculpture; tonality, melody and harmony in music; grace in dance; and structure, coherence and meaning in the written arts. Most of these artists couldn't get arrested when it came to making a living with their "outdated" art, so they taught. Few young would-be artists at the time were interested, but enough of them did learn the basics, and they are now professionals, coming of age to revitalize traditional art forms with a contemporary sensibility. There is enormous energy buzzing through the art world because of this new life. Not only painters and sculptors but novelists, poets, and composers, too, are reaching back to the best of the past for inspiration that will help them contemporize the verities of life that remain particularly and eternally relevant to our time and place.

America's stage is now set for a second renaissance, both philosophically and artistically, the critical combination. As

European culture and art was the result of the finest of Greek and Roman achievement, and the political formation of America was a result of the best of European intellectual achievement, so may we now become *cultural* producers ourselves in the one realm left to complete the circle of progress. It is our turn, now, to *advance* the ideological tenets that the Greeks first identified nearly three thousand years ago in philosophy and in art. The whole world is scrambling to share in the material benefits made possible through our marrying science and political/economic liberty. Now it falls to us to take leadership in the philosophical/artistic arenas and offer an earthly humanistic spiritual component to life's exalted experiences as well.

Against all odds, we must not repeat the past. The genius of the European Renaissance leaders was that they selected fundamentals from Greek philosophy and made them their own: David, not Apollo. Now in this brilliant scientific age that permits travel to outer space routinely, the time has come for us to initiate a journey into inner space—the humanities— to discover a deeper, rational understanding of man as a spiritual creature who *needs* access to the profound meanings of life here on earth, meanings that flow from philosophy to the arts, from the arts to the culture as a whole. What will the next millennium hero and heroine look like?—yes, we're in desperate need of heroes again. At this late date it may be that art is the only dynamic powerful and immediate enough to arouse individuals of all persuasions to the notion that the world can be beautiful and men and women can achieve their best—imagine what Hollywood and TV could create with *these* themes! The time for angst, anger and alienation (and action for the sake of action!) is past and passé. The time for philosopher-kings is long gone. But the time for philosopher-artists is *now*.

Every genuine work of art has as much reason for being as the earth and the sun.

Ralph Waldo Emerson

Sharing the Miracle

First published in ART Ideas, *Spring 1995.*

I knew the process, of course. Intellectually. From sculptor's clay model to rubber mold to wax to ceramic mold and...at last, *cire perdue*, the dramatic (I imagined) pouring of the bronze—the method of casting bronze sculpture through the ancient "lost wax" method that was brought to its apotheosis during ancient Greece, revived during the Renaissance and continues today. I even understood and was completely at home with the finer points of bringing a work of bronze from conception to completion: from the maquette (the artist's "sketch") and the armature that becomes the skeleton supporting the articulated clay model to the chasing and patination that fine tune and color the finished bronze piece. I had seen countless clay models "in the works" by various sculptors, revisited many of the same pieces again after they had been cast in plaster, and finally viewed the finished bronzes. But I had never witnessed with my own eyes the actual pouring of the bronze.

For years, I'd begged every sculptor I knew to take me along to the foundry when next they went. I promised to stay out of the way. I even promised to keep quiet. I promised lunch, dinner...anything. Just take me to see it! I wasn't hurt when no invitation ever came my way. I knew well that the sculptors I entreated—even though some of them were close friends as well as colleagues—were totally and properly absorbed with their work. Most of them, although they often execute detail work on the wax model, chasing on the finished bronze, and routinely supervise the patination process, don't habitually watch the actual pouring of the bronze themselves, even when their own molds are being filled. Any remembrance of my request at any of the crucial points in their work requiring a foundry visit was understandably wiped away by whatever existential task demanded their attention at the time. Sculptors have work to do when they go to a foundry.

Living in New York, I could have gone "cold" to any one of a number of respectable foundries that offer public tours of their facilities. But, stubbornly, I didn't want an impersonal lecture tour, and I also didn't want to be part of a group. Sculpture is a major passion with me; therefore, I held out. I resolutely desired to be the only civilian in the room (the place? the space? where *was* it?) when *it* happened. Time passed. I pined on.

Then I made a new friend (through ART) who was, over time, to become a soul brother. And his first act of friendship was to offer me a whole day of sculpture-related events and art/ideas conversation, a day holding as its centerpiece that singular experience I had longed for—a private viewing of my first bronze pouring. My sculptor friend did not even plan to parlay our visit to the foundry by tending to any of his own work on the appointed day; the pouring was a gift from him to me, and I accepted it as such. Excited and grateful, I was certain that an important occasion was about to take place. How wrong I was! "Important" would be a puny word, indeed, to characterize what was to become one of the supreme spiritual experiences of my life.

The head of the foundry (and since then its owner) showed his respect for my sculptor friend—his client—by escorting me personally into his domain. An attractive, compact man vital with energy, my guide's silver white hair and trim beard of the same color served only to frame his intelligent, brown eyes, eyes that—serious or laughing—emitted a fire consistent with his profession. Well before our first handshake or his first words of welcome, I was intensely aware of those eyes, lit from deep inside him. Here was a man in love with his work. Now we were *three* kindred spirits venturing forth together on this mutually chosen morning.

Passing from the carpeted public sculpture gallery down a hallway lined with comfortably decorated offices, a door was opened to let me enter first into the foundry proper. The contrast was startling. I suddenly heard the heels of my boots clicking over bare concrete floors. I smelled a potpourri of unfamiliar chemicals, traced the purposeful strides of people dressed for messy jobs, and heard dozens of sounds, none of which I could positively identify. A crossing had been made: I had traversed a threshold into a known but heretofore unseen world, into the active midst of a working factory as utilitarian as any other that might manufacture mere widgets. But here, it was *art* they were making. Here, artists and artisans worked together every day plying the highly skilled crafts that technically produce the art of bronze sculpture. Sculpture, that puissant three-dimensional, sensuously tangible form of art with the power not only to evoke emotional responses ranging from joy to sorrow in us but also to entice us to touch it, to stroke it, to physically handle it as well. For me, the homely and cracked factory floor upon which our trio so casually tread, chatting and pointing, became as holy ground...the laborers, workers of wonders. The sense of commitment and camaraderie I had observed in my guide—the boss—permeated every room we entered. Employees of different ages, colors, genders, sizes and ranks exhibited the same focus and friendliness that he did. The foundry mark stamped onto every piece of sculpture leaving this place (whether the art be monumental or modest) bears witness to the cooperation and pride of all those responsible for making it a fine mark.

I had many questions. Some, I suppose, were posed in rather tedious detail. But all were answered seriously and patiently. My friend, I noticed, remained rather quiet, letting the foundryman take front and center. I looked and listened and learned. And marvelled. I already knew that this method of casting bronze sculpture had been going on for nearly three thousand years, but I had no idea how modern technology has altered and improved the process. I heard the enchanting story of how, after their lunch break, the Italian Renaissance workers used to flip their empty wine bottle into the molten bronze just prior to a pour. I learned that the exercise wasn't a frivolous flourish; the property of silicon in the glass of the bottle actually strengthened the metal. Today, after many years of neglecting the practice, silicon is again added (albeit less romantically) to the bronze, which is otherwise an alloy of copper, lead, tin and zinc.

Surrounded by plaster models of sundry shapes and scale, I watched, mesmerized, as melted, orange-colored wax was brushed swiftly and expertly onto the inside surface of rubber molds that had been pulled from plaster casts. The casts, themselves, had been made from an earlier, less sturdy rubber mold taken directly from the original clay model. Certain contemporary sculptors bypass the plaster phase and go straight from clay to the production mold which gives the finished work a rougher texture, but most elect to make a plaster cast for two reasons: one, they can work the plaster itself to refine a piece and, two, since the clay model is usually damaged by taking a mold from it, they have a more durable model from which to pull future molds in case the first one is destroyed. I noted that the wax was being layered onto the mold more thinly than I had expected, perhaps only 1/8 to 1/4 inch thick in all, depending on the size of the piece. It was astonishing to realize that when the mold is removed, it is this fragile wall of wax, cooled into a hollow form identical to the original clay model, on which (as mentioned earlier) many sculptors do even more detail work to assure that it is precisely as they wish it. Whether done by the artist or a skilled artisan at the foundry, this last touching-up of the wax is crucial because it is *this* wax form that will be "lost" when the final ceramic mold built around it receives the flow of liquid bronze that ultimately assumes the wax's shape as it takes its physical place to become a work of art.

Once we left the room containing the plaster casts, nothing really resembling "art" presented itself again for a good long while. I saw wax gates and vents attached to the wax sculptural forms that would eventually provide the wax and gases their exit routes out of the mold. Then I saw the forms fitted with metal funnels that would become the entry points into which the bronze would flow to fill the vacated spaces. I saw the ceramic molds (modern space technology permitting this new material to withstand levels of high heat undreamed of in past eras) tonged white-hot from huge kilns and placed casually in haphazard rows to cool like any other piece of pottery, as if each piece of ceramic didn't contain the precious, now empty core that would soon make way for art. I sensed a growing inner anticipation that, increasingly, began to shorten my questions. The *piece de resistance* came next, and I was far from resisting. Only minutes later, the foundryman checked his watch—they weren't pouring just for me; there *was* a schedule. It was time.

Entering the pouring room was entering a furnace. The referred heat from the boiling cauldron of bronze dictated our physical distance from the scene about to be played or, rather, it seemed to me, the rite to be performed. Even the three workmen present—dressed in high black boots, long silver asbestos coats, thick gray gloves, and yellow hard hats with clear, acrylic full-face visors—looked like modern medieval practitioners about to enact a ritual. A huge rectangular tub partially filled with sand stood at center stage. With their bases planted carefully into the sand, dozens of ceramic molds stood upended, ready to be filled with the bronze. If the molds toppled, or even tipped, during the pouring, all would be lost. Every movement, every action of the men was calm but precise and measured. An accident could mean not only the destruction of the art but of their own lives. Behind them all, waiting to be shaped to the will of an artist's vision, the golden bronze bubbled. It looked as if the source of all life, the sun itself, had liquefied its energy and streamed into the crucible.

Surveying the different shapes of the ceramic vessels into which the hot metal would soon flow, I was struck by the obvious realization that the bronze that would fill these vessels had no will of its own. If it spilled, it would cool into random patterns depending on gravity and obstacles diverting its indiscriminate path. If the ceramic mold into which it was poured contained ugliness of physical shape or evil of philosophical content, the bronze would cool to become a tangible and concrete manifestation of the mind and soul of the man or woman who had wished to make permanent that image and those ideas. If the vessel contained beauty of shape and nobility of spirit, that, too, would immortalize the soul of the artist who had created it. The bronze, itself a man-invented combination of nature's elements, would be molded forever into an eternal testament to the human will that shaped it.

All three of us were suddenly, unexpectedly, quiet. The only sound was that of the molten metal, coming to a level of heat that now sent occasional droplets of liquid flying up from its roiling surface to flash through the air like a handful of gold coins tossed out in wild abandon. In the background, we could discern the soft-shoe shuffling and vocal murmurs of the men preparing to lift the caldron into the contraption used for the actual pouring. Eventually, one man guided the contraption itself into position, and the other two, maneuvering handles at opposite ends of a long pole at the center of which hung the suspended cauldron, began to pour the bronze that looked and flowed like liquid fire into the separate ceramic molds, inch by inch, one by one.

Disconnected images swirled together in my mind: Prometheus stealing fire from the gods, risking wrath and wounds to offer his gift to humankind, and man taming that fire to make this moment possible—this moment as the smoldering bronze liquid continued to flow from the crucible as benignly as sweet honey from a jar; Athena, protector of the arts...and of heroes, born like an idea in full bloom from Zeus's head to offer her wisdom to the great heroes of the past...and to us, too, if we would earn it. To save a life is heroic, indeed; to give life can also be heroic, but to give life *meaning* in the sense of creating from the mind an object of worth is the most heroic of all. I surrendered now to the heroic triumph of the pouring of the bronze. To its possibilities. To the triumph of every artist who loves life enough to conceive an internal idea worth giving external shape. I felt like kneeling to those artists, whoever and wherever they are...or whoever they may have been. But I felt like rising, too, from the pride of knowing that I shared the visions of the best of them and that, in responding to their work, I completed the circle of creation. Objects created by individuals, the sublime force of a human *intention* being turned into concrete form—the human ability and desire to create an enduring entity from the molten bronze being poured out now before me in such a minutely controlled fashion that I could scarcely believe those brave workmen breathed at all so steady was their rhythm while executing a process that could destroy them if they slipped—an exhilarating but sobering process that, by nature of its components' complete malleability to human purpose, can be turned equally to death and destruction or to celebration and joy. So danger *was* part of it. *The creation despite the danger*. The uncertainty—the risk—that all serious sculptors are willing to bear, all poets, composers, painters and novelists each time they create a work of art, all scientists when they create a new invention—the dangers, mental and physical, tried and met for the sake of the creation. Let it be worthy!

I felt a serene and abiding oneness with the whole world at that moment, a union of mind, body and soul born from the joy of living to witness such a sight of creation, a harmony shared with all others present that day or far away and unknown to me who share the values that make such an experience one of the spirit. I did not know that I was weeping until I glanced at my friend who I saw, smiling gently at me, held tears of his own barely in check. Then I turned to my guide, whose lively brown eyes brimmed, too, as he gazed kindly into mine with an expression so intimate it was an embrace. I heard my friend's voice, as if coming to me from a great distance, saying something about going for a tissue. "My first time..." I stammered stupidly. The brown eyes of the foundryman held mine steadily for one instant more, while he shook his head. "No," he said simply. "I feel it every time."

Suddenly the moment was shattered by streaks of blazing red and gold bursting like fireworks and exploding like bombs as the bronze—unleashed, now—gushed through a rupture in one of the large ceramic molds. I jumped back in the same instant the foundryman leaped forward. "Breakthrough!" he shouted as he raced to help. Erupting like scalding lava from a miniature volcano, the bronze surged out and splashed in all directions, increasing the fury of its speed as the crack in the vessel enlarged second by second into a gaping hole. In another instant I knew it would blow out of its remaining confines altogether. But the men were running toward it now, having grabbed fistfuls of wet mud from an emergency pile nearby; as a team, they slathered the substance over the opening to stop it up until the mold could contain the bronze once more. The workers layered the mud around the split with their heavy gloves; the foundryman worked barehanded.

It was over as quickly as it had begun. My sculptor friend arrived with tissues in hand just as the last flames seemed to re-enter the mold, while the last wild jets of loose lava spent themselves out crawling in still-burning but no longer spreading masses to a slow halt on the concrete floor. "A breakthrough?" he asked incredulously. I nodded, stunned. He did not try to hide the disappointment in his voice. "In all my years, I've never seen one," he said.

Later, the three of us, walking on together but each alone for many moments with our own private thoughts, passed by dozens of open shelves holding a myriad of recently cast work. No matter what the subject matter (if any) all pieces stood in the same rough state in which they had emerged from the same type of ceramic molds we had just seen receiving the liquid bronze. After the cooling down period which allows the bronze to resolidify, the molds had been broken to release the fresh castings. Metal rods remained sticking out from caked bronze lumps, some twisted so brutally by the trauma of heat and pressure that they looked like mutilated branches hanging desperately onto alien and inhospitable bushes. None of it remotely resembled art. I broke the silence. "I feel happy to have seen the breakthrough," I ventured. "At the time I didn't realize how rare that is." The foundryman frowned. "Well, I'm not happy. We lost art—that piece was ruined—and we lost money. We could have lost more. No one was hurt, but..." His voice trailed off.

By the time we reached the second floor, all of us had regained our equilibrium. Here, I saw artisans finishing and chasing every imaginable shape from an ethereal female nude to porpoises and funny-looking creatures defying description. Here I saw the dull, lumpy surfaces from casts like the ones downstairs becoming art again for the first time since I viewed the plasters earlier in the morning. Some of the nearly-completed pieces moved me, most did not. Some I did not consider art at all. At this I was neither disappointed nor surprised; our culture is not one where we can encounter artistic excellence often. I did admire enormously the wielding of torches in the room where highly skilled men and women applied acids to the bronze surfaces—a delicate and demanding craft—to create the exact color of patina desired by each artist. The polishing room was last, where, finally, I could study the end results of the complex and arduous process that is bronze sculpture casting. Smooth and gleaming images that had begun—how long ago?—in the imaginative privacy of the sculptors' minds who had envisioned them now sat on long tables, finished completely and ready to enter the world with a life of their own. It was amazing to think that these images were physically, after all, nothing more than shapes of metal, and hollow at that. Some larger pieces were even completely open at the bottom so that, when turned over, I could see nothing more than an empty cavern of bumpy bronze. But when set aright again, the image had the absolute power, by stimulating my psycho-sensory value system, to affect me in the most profound, emotional manner. It seemed a miracle. Art *is* a miracle. A miracle of the human mind incarnate.

Our hands clasped not in goodbye nor in a thank you but as a gesture of understanding that no words could express.

The foundryman who loved his work—my guide—returned to his beloved territory alone. My friend and I went on to lunch, to examine and to discuss other sculpture, to talk of art and ideas as only soulmates can do. That day—his gift—will remain with me always.

As I lay in bed that night, mulling it all over before sleep turned my experience into a memory, I couldn't help thinking about what men and women have wrought throughout the ages. What shapes and sounds and stories we have created! From a chunk of clay, a block of stone, a palette of paint, a pot full of metal, a thimble full of chemicals, a world full of nature's bounties, all to be recreated into tangible manifestations of human ideas. Matter reshaped by human reason, will and desire to serve and bring pleasure to the human mind, body and soul—this was the *essence* of the miracle of the pouring of the bronze. Recreating by a process of compatible combination the raw matter of the physical world and the abstract ideas from our minds into art and inventions that cause us to stand in awe of *ourselves*...our joys, our tears, our hopes, our intellects, our abilities and all that still waits—the possibilities—for future reshaping into the endless frozen forms of ideas...especially the forms of fine art, which nurture our souls as well as our minds. Every act of creation, in its own way, seems a miracle to behold, of course. But, surely, by evidence of the most beautiful and noble and life-enriching acts of human creation—art—we, ourselves, become the most miraculous creations of all.